JAMESTOWN  EDUCA

English, Yes!

Learning English Through Literature

Level 6: Advanced

 **Glencoe**

New York, New York   Columbus, Ohio   Chicago, Illinois   Peoria, Illinois   Woodland Hills, California

JAMESTOWN EDUCATION

Cover photo illustration: Third Eye Image/Solus Photography/Veer.

 **Glencoe**

The **McGraw·Hill** Companies

Send all inquiries to:
Glencoe/McGraw-Hill
8787 Orion Place
Columbus, OH 43240-4027

ISBN 0-07-831115-2
Printed in the United States of America
1 2 3 4 5 6 7 8 9 10 021 08 07 06 05 04 03

CONTENTS

ACKNOWLEDGMENTS

Acknowledgment is gratefully made to the following publishers, authors, and agents for permission to reprint these works. Adaptations and/or abridgments are by Burton Goodman.

"Talking in the New Land." Excerpted and adapted from *Talking in the New Land* by Edite Cunhã. Reprinted by permission of the author.

"The Force of Luck." Adapted with permission of the Museum of New Mexico Press, from *Cuentos: Tales from the Hispanic Southwest* by José Griego y Maestas and Rudolfo Anaya. Based on stories originally collected by Juan B. Rael. Copyright © 1980 Museum of New Mexico Press.

"Sixteen" by Maureen Daly. Copyright © 1972 by Scholastic Magazine Inc. Reprinted by permission of Scholastic Inc.

"Alone." From *Oh Pray My Wings Are Gonna Fit Me Well* by Maya Angelou. Copyright © 1975 by Maya Angelou. Reprinted by permission of Random House Inc.

"The Sanctuary," adapted from "The Sanctuary Desolated" by Jesse Stuart. Copyright by Jesse Stuart and the Jesse Stuart Foundation. Reprinted by permission of The Jesse Stuart Foundation, P.O. Box 391, Ashland, KY 41114.

"Lineage" by Margaret Walker from *This Is My Century: New and Collected Poems*. Copyright © 1989 by Margaret Walker Alexander. Used by permission of The University of Georgia Press.

"The Courage That My Mother Had" by Edna St. Vincent Millay. From *Collected Poems*, HarperCollins. Copyright © 1954, 1982 by Norma Millay Ellis. Reprinted by permission of Elizabeth Barnett, literary executor.

"The Surveyor." Reprinted with the permission of Atheneum Books for Young Readers, an imprint of Simon & Schuster, from *Where the Flame Trees Bloom* by Alma Flor Ada. Text copyright © 1994 Alma Flor Ada.

JAMESTOWN EDUCATION

English, Yes!

Learning English Through Literature

Level 6: Advanced

TALKING IN THE NEW LAND

based on a story by Edite Cunhã

Connections

Study the picture on the left. Describe what you see.

- Notice the girl sitting on the chair. Where is she? Who else is in the room? What do you think the girl is thinking?

- Who are the two adults at the bottom of the picture? What do you think the man is thinking? How does he feel?

- Read the title of the story. What new information does it add to what you learned from the illustration?

- Do you have good memories of a time when you were as young as the girl in the picture? Describe these memories.

As you read, think about how the picture connects to the story.

Words to Learn

In this story, you will learn some new words. You will also learn an *idiom*. An idiom is a group of words that together mean something quite different from what they mean separately. For example, the idiom *hand over* means "give to someone."

TALKING IN THE NEW LAND

based on a story by Edite Cunhã

No one was as stubborn as Pa.

Before I started school in America I was Edite. Maria Edite dos Anjos Cunhã. I loved my name. I'd say, "Maria Edite dos Anjos Cunhã" whenever I could. My name was musical and beautiful. And through it I knew exactly who I was.

When I was seven, we moved from our little house in Sobreira, Portugal, to Peabody, Massachusetts. I was in America for about a week when, one morning, someone took me to school and handed me over to the teacher, Mrs. Donahue.

Mrs. Donahue spoke Portuguese, an amazing thing, I thought, for a woman with such a funny name, one so difficult to pronounce. *"Como é que te chamas?"*[1] she asked me as she led me to a desk by a big window.

"Maria Edite dos Anjos Cunhã," I recited, staring at Mrs. Donahue, as I wondered how a woman with that name could speak my language.

In fact, Mrs. Donahue was Portuguese. She was a Silva. But she had married a man named Donahue and had changed her name. She changed my name, too, on the first day of school.

"Your name will be Mary Edith Cunhã," she announced. "In America you need only two or three names. Mary Edith is a lovely name. And it will be easier to pronounce."

My name was Ed*ite*. *Maria Edite*. Maria Edite dos Anjos Cunhã. *I* had no trouble pronouncing it.

"Mary Edith, Ed*ithhh*, Mary *Edithhh*," Mrs. Donahue said. She wrinkled up her nose and raised her upper lip to show me the proper place to put the tongue to make the *th* sound. She looked hideous and there was a big pain in my head. I wanted to scream

1. *Como é que te chamas?:* What's your name?

out my real name. But I knew I couldn't argue with her.

At home I cried and cried. Ma and Pa wanted to know about my day at school. I tried to explain, but I couldn't pronounce the new name for them.

Day after day Mrs. Donahue made me practice pronouncing the name that wasn't mine. Mary Ed*ithhhhh*. Mary Ed*ithhh*. Mary Ed*ithhh*! Weeks later I still wouldn't respond when she called it out in class.

She was a tiny woman, Mrs. Donahue, not much bigger than I was. Her gray hair was always cut short, and she wore a smile on her face almost every day. It was not a big, broad smile. It was hardly visible. But it was there, in her eyes, and at the corners of her mouth. She usually wore suits with jackets neatly fitted at the waist. On her feet she wore black leather shoes, tightly laced. The shoes matched each other, but they were not identical. One of them had a very thick sole because one of Mrs. Donahue's legs was shorter than the other.

I grew to love Mrs. Donahue, and she helped me learn English. She was the only teacher at school who danced with us. She thought that it was important to dance. Every day after recess she took us all to the big open space at the back of the room. We stood in a circle and joined hands. Mrs. Donahue would hum a high note and we became a twirling, singing wheel. Mrs. Donahue hobbled on her short leg and sang out, "Here we go, loop-de-loop." We took three steps, then a pause. Her last "loop" was always very high. It seemed to squeak above our heads, bouncing on the ceiling. "Here we go, loop-de-lie." Three more steps, another pause, and on we whirled.

"Here we go, loop-de-loop." Pause. "All on a Saturday night." To anyone looking in from the corridor we were surely a very interesting sight, a circle of children of different sizes and colors singing and twirling with our tiny hobbling teacher.

When I was nine, Pa went to an auction and bought a big house on Tremont Street. We moved in the spring. The lawn at the side of the house dipped downward in a gentle slope and was covered with a thick, dense row of tall lilac bushes. I soon discovered that I could crawl between the bushes and hide from my brothers in the fragrant, sweet-smelling shade. It was paradise.

I was mostly wild and joyful on Tremont Street. But now and then there was a shadow that fell over my days.

"Oh, *Ediiiite! Ediiiite!*" Since Pa didn't speak English very well, he always called me, without the least bit of warning, to be his voice. He expected me to drop whatever I was doing to take care of something. Pa never called my brother, Carlos. No, Carlos never had to do anything but play! Recently, I'd had to talk on the telephone to a woman who wanted some old dishes. The dishes, along with a lot of old furniture and junk, had been in the house when we moved in. They were in the cellar, stacked in cardboard boxes and covered with dust. The woman called many times, wanting to speak with Pa.

"My father can't speak English," I would say. "He says to tell you that the dishes are in our house and they belong to us." But she did not seem to understand. Every few days she would call.

"Oh, *Ediiiite!*" Pa's voice echoed through the empty rooms. I wanted to pretend I had not heard it when it had that tone. But I couldn't escape. I couldn't disappear into thin air as I wished to do at such times.

"*Ediiiite!*" Yes, that tone was certainly there. Pa was calling me to do something only I could do. What was it now? Did I have to talk to the insurance company? They were always using words I couldn't understand: premium and dividend. That made me nervous.

"Please wait. I call my daughter," Pa was saying. He was talking to someone, someone in the house. Who could it be?

"Oh, *Ediiiite!*"

"*Que éééé?*"[2]

"*Come over here and talk to this lady.*"

Reluctantly, I walked through the empty rooms toward the kitchen. Through the kitchen door I could see a slim lady dressed in

2. *Que éééé?:* What is it?

brown standing at the top of the stairs. She had on high-heeled shoes and was holding a brown purse. As soon as Pa saw me he said to me, *"See what she wants."*

The lady had dark hair that was very smooth. The ends of it flipped up in a way that I liked.

"Hello. I'm the lady who called about the dishes."

I stared at her without a word. My stomach turned over.

"What did she say?" Pa wanted to know.

"She says she's the lady who wants the dishes."

Pa's face hardened some.

"Tell her she's wasting her time. We're not giving them to her. Didn't you already tell her that on the telephone?"

I nodded, standing helplessly between them.

"Well, tell her again." Pa was getting angry. I wanted to disappear.

"My father says he can't give you the dishes," I said to the lady. She clutched her purse and leaned a little forward.

"Yes, you told me that on the phone. But I wanted to come in person and speak with your father because it's very important to me that—"

"My father can't speak English," I interrupted her. Why didn't she just go away?

"Yes, I understand that. But I wanted to see him." She looked at Pa, who was standing in the doorway to the kitchen holding his hammer. The kitchen was up one step from the porch. Pa was a small man, but he looked kind of scary staring down at us like that.

"What is she saying?"

"She says she wanted to talk to you about getting her dishes."

"Tell her the dishes are ours. They were in the house. We bought the house and everything in it. Tell her the lawyer said so."

The lady was looking at me hopefully.

"My father says the dishes are ours because we bought the house and the lawyer said everything in the house is ours now."

"Yes, I know that, but I was away when the house was being sold. I didn't know . . ."

There were footsteps on the stairs behind her. It was Ma coming up from the second floor to find out what was going on. The lady moved away from the door to let Ma in.

"This is my wife," Pa said to the lady. The lady said hello to Ma, who smiled and nodded her head. She looked at me, then at Pa in a questioning way.

"It's the lady who wants our dishes," Pa explained.

Ma looked at her again and smiled, but I could tell she was a little worried.

We stood there in kind of a funny circle; the lady looked at each of us in turn and took a deep breath.

"I didn't know," she continued, "that the dishes were in the house. I was away. They are very important to me. They belonged to my grandmother. I'd really like to get them back." She spoke this while looking back and forth between Ma and Pa. Then she looked down at me, leaning forward again. "Will you tell your parents, please?"

I spoke in a hurry to get the words out.

"She said she didn't know the dishes were in the house because she was away. They were her grandmother's dishes, and she wants them back." I felt deep sorrow at the thought of the lady returning home to find her grandmother's dishes sold.

"We don't need all those dishes. Let's give them to her," Ma said in her calm way. I felt relieved. We could give the lady the dishes and she would go away. But Pa got angry.

"I already said what I had to say. The dishes are ours. That is all."

"Pa, she said she didn't know. They were her grandmother's dishes. She needs to have them." I was speaking wildly and loud now. The lady looked at me questioningly, but I didn't want to speak to her again.

"She's only saying that to trick us. If she wanted those dishes she should have taken them out before the house was sold. Tell her we are not fools. Tell her to forget it. She can go away. Tell her not to call or come here again."

"What is he saying?" The lady was looking at me again.

I ignored her. I felt sorry for Pa for always feeling that people were trying to trick him. I wanted him to trust people. I wanted the lady to have her grandmother's dishes. I closed my eyes and willed myself away.

"Tell her what I said!" Pa yelled.

"Pa, just give her the dishes! They were her grandmother's dishes!" My voice cracked as I yelled back at him. Tears were rising in my eyes.

I hated Pa for being so stubborn. I hated the lady for not taking the dishes before the house was sold. And I hated myself because I had to tell her that she couldn't have her grandmother's dishes.

Put an *x* in the box next to the correct answer.

Reading Comprehension

1. How old was Edite when her family moved to Massachusetts?
   - ❏ **a.** five years old
   - ❏ **b.** seven years old
   - ❏ **c.** nine years old

2. Edite was surprised that Mrs. Donahue
   - ❏ **a.** could speak Portuguese.
   - ❏ **b.** was so tall.
   - ❏ **c.** didn't like to dance.

3. Edite was unhappy because Mrs. Donahue
   - ❏ **a.** didn't like her.
   - ❏ **b.** wouldn't help her learn English.
   - ❏ **c.** changed her name to Mary Edith.

4. Edite's father sometimes asked Edite for help because he
   - ❏ **a.** was not very strong.
   - ❏ **b.** was usually very busy.
   - ❏ **c.** didn't speak English very well.

5. The lady in brown said that the dishes belonged to her
   - ❏ **a.** daughter.
   - ❏ **b.** grandmother.
   - ❏ **c.** mother.

6. Which statement is true?
   - ❏ **a.** Pa thought that the lady was trying to trick him.
   - ❏ **b.** Edite wanted the dishes.
   - ❏ **c.** Ma told the lady she couldn't have the dishes.

Vocabulary

7. Mrs. Donahue's shoes matched, but they were not identical. The word *identical* means
   - ❏ **a.** beautiful.
   - ❏ **b.** small.
   - ❏ **c.** exactly alike.

8. When Mrs. Donahue raised her upper lip, Edite thought she looked hideous. The word *hideous* means
   - ❏ **a.** very ugly.
   - ❏ **b.** very pretty.
   - ❏ **c.** very sad.

9. She clutched a purse in her hand. The word *clutched* means
   - ❏ **a.** looked at.
   - ❏ **b.** held tightly.
   - ❏ **c.** dropped.

Idioms

10. Edite was handed over to the teacher. The idiom *to hand over* means
    - ❏ **a.** to hold someone's hand.
    - ❏ **b.** to give to another.
    - ❏ **c.** to be afraid.

How many questions did you answer correctly? Circle your score. Then fill in your score on the Score Chart on page 184.

Number Correct	1	2	3	4	5	6	7	8	9	10
Score	10	20	30	40	50	60	70	80	90	100

Exercise A

Understanding the story. Answer each question with a complete sentence. You may look back at the story. The first one has been done for you.

1. How old was Edite when she moved to Massachusetts?

   Edite was seven years old.

2. Where did Edite live before she came to America?

   _____

3. What name did Mrs. Donahue give to Edite?

   _____

4. Why did one of Mrs. Donahue's shoes have a very thick sole?

   _____

5. Why did Edite have to be her father's "voice"?

   _____

   _____

6. What did the lady come to the house to get?

   _____

   _____

7. Where were the dishes?

   _____

8. Why did Edite hate the lady?

   _____

   _____

Exercise B

Adding vocabulary. On the left are 8 words from the story. Complete each sentence by adding the correct word. The first one has been done for you.

pretend

echoed

reluctantly

stubborn

hobbled

musical

visible

fragrant

1. Pa refused to listen to anyone because he was

    very ____*stubborn*____.

2. Edite thought that her name sounded

    _____ and beautiful.

3. Since one of Mrs. Donahue's legs was shorter than

    the other, she _____ when she

    walked.

4. Mrs. Donahue usually had a smile on her face.

    However, it was not a big smile; it was hardly

    _____.

5. Sometimes Edite wanted to

    _____ that she didn't hear her

    father's voice.

6. The lilac bushes smelled very sweet; they were

    _____.

7. Pa's voice bounced off the walls and

    _____ through the empty rooms.

8. Edite didn't want to talk to the lady; she spoke to

    her _____.

Exercise C

Adding punctuation. The following passage needs **punctuation marks**. Add capital letters, periods, question marks, commas, and quotation marks. Then write the corrected passage on the lines below.

edite walked to the kitchen she saw a lady who was wearing a brown dress the lady looked at edite and said do you think i can have the dishes

edite asked if you wanted the dishes why did you leave them in the house

the lady answered i was away when the house was sold i didn't know the dishes were still there

_____

_____

_____

_____

_____

_____

_____

_____

_____

_____

_____

_____

Exercise D

Finding synonyms. Read each sentence. Then select the **synonym** (the word most similar in meaning) for the word in capital letters. Circle the letter of the correct answer. Each capitalized word appears in the story. The first one has been done for you.

1. Edite thought that her name was easy to pronounce.

    PRONOUNCE **(a.)** say **b.** change **c.** forget

2. Sometimes, Edite didn't respond when the teacher called her Mary Edith.

    RESPOND **a.** cry **b.** answer **c.** leave

3. Mrs. Donahue showed Edite the proper place to put her tongue to make the *th* sound.

    PROPER **a.** correct **b.** wrong **c.** funny

4. The children went twirling round and round in a circle as they danced.

    TWIRLING **a.** listening **b.** resting **c.** spinning

5. The dishes were stacked in boxes in the basement.

    STACKED **a.** washed **b.** piled **c.** broken

6. Pa looked scary as he stood there with a hammer in his hand.

    SCARY **a.** cheerful **b.** friendly **c.** frightening

7. Edite was filled with sorrow when she realized that the lady wasn't going to get the dishes.

    SORROW **a.** sadness **b.** happiness **c.** interest

8. Edite was very happy on Tremont Street; to her it was paradise.

    PARADISE **a.** near **b.** sunny **c.** heaven

Exercise E

Part A

Building sentences. Combine two **simple sentences** into one **compound sentence** by using a comma and the **coordinating conjunction** in parentheses (*and* or *but*). Write the compound sentence on the line. The first one has been done for you.

1. Edite was born in Portugal. She moved to America. (but)

   Edite was born in Portugal, but she moved to America.

2. Mrs. Donahue was named Silva. She changed her name. (but)

   _____

   _____

3. Edite's teacher was Mrs. Donahue. She spoke Portuguese. (and)

   _____

   _____

4. The teacher thought Edite's name was hard to pronounce. Edite had no trouble pronouncing it. (but)

   _____

   _____

   _____

5. Mrs. Donahue usually wore suits. She always wore black leather shoes. (and)

   _____

   _____

6. Edite wanted to keep her real name. She couldn't argue with Mrs. Donahue. (but)

   _____

   _____

7. Edite's father bought a house. The family moved there in the spring. (and)

_____

_____

8. Edite told the woman not to call back. The woman didn't listen to Edite. (but)

_____

_____

9. Edite wanted her father to trust people. He didn't listen to her. (but)

_____

_____

10. Edite hated her father for being so stubborn. She hated the lady for not taking the dishes. (and)

_____

_____

_____

Part B

By combining **simple sentences** into **compound sentences**, you can make your writing stronger and more interesting. The following passage contains 8 simple sentences.

Pa bought a house on Tremont Street. The family moved there. Usually Edite was happy. One thing bothered her. Pa didn't speak English very well. He often asked her to be "his voice." Edite did not like to do this. She always helped him.

Combine the 8 simple sentences into 4 compound sentences by using commas with the conjunctions *but* or *and*. Write the new passage on the lines below.

_____

_____

_____

_____

_____

_____

_____

_____

_____

_____

_____

_____

_____

_____

_____

Exercise F

Vocabulary review. Write a complete sentence for each word.

1. hideous _____

_____

2. identical _____

_____

3. clutched _____

_____

4. stubborn _____

_____

5. visible _____

_____

6. pretend _____

_____

7. reluctantly _____

_____

8. pronounce _____

_____

9. respond _____

_____

10. fragrant _____

_____

SHARING WITH OTHERS

This section provides you with opportunities to share your thoughts and ideas with others, while you practice and improve your reading, writing, speaking, and listening skills.

Part A

Discuss the following questions. Share your answers with your partner or with the group.

1. Why did Mrs. Donahue change Edite's name? Explain why you approve or disapprove of what Mrs. Donahue did.

2. Edite said that through her name she knew exactly who she was. What did Edite mean by that? Why did changing her name cause Edite so much pain?

3. Eventually, Edite grew to love Mrs. Donahue. Why do you think that happened? Is Mrs. Donahue the kind of person you think you would like? Why?

4. Why was Edite so uncomfortable when she was talking to the lady? Give at least three reasons.

5. Edite complained that she had to help her father, while her brother, Carlos, spent all his time playing. Do you think that was true? Why? Children often complain about being treated unfairly. Have you ever been in that situation? Explain.

6. Should Pa have given the dishes to the lady? Why?

7. New situations can be very frightening. Do you remember your first day in a new school, class, or country? Tell about your experience.

8. "Talking in the New Land" is a true story. Does this surprise you? Why?

Part B

1. Take a few moments to think about your name. Consider the following: How did you get your name? Do you like your name? Has your name changed over time? Does your name have any special meaning? If you could change your name, would you do that? If so, what name would you choose? Do you have a nickname?

On the lines below, write three sentences about your name.

a. _____

_____

_____

b. _____

_____

_____

c. _____

_____

_____

Suppose you were writing a **paragraph** about your name. What would the **topic sentence** be? Write it below. (Remember, a topic sentence gives the main idea of a paragraph.)

_____

_____

_____

_____

_____

_____

2. Write a paragraph to answer Question 6. Begin the paragraph with one of these **topic sentences**:

> I think that Pa should have given the dishes to the lady.
> I think that Pa was right to keep the dishes.

Be sure to give reasons to support your opinion.

_____

_____

_____

_____

_____

_____

_____

_____

_____

_____

_____

_____

_____

_____

_____

_____

_____

_____

KEESH

based on a story by Jack London

Connections

Study the picture on the left. Describe what you see.

- Where does this story take place? How can you tell?
- What is the bear doing? What is the young man doing?
- Do you think this will be an exciting story? Why or why not?
- Do you have a favorite adventure story? Tell about it.

As you read, think about how the picture connects to the story.

Words to Learn

In this story, you will learn some new words. You will also learn some *idioms*. For example, *to keep an eye on* is an idiom that means "to watch."

KEESH

based on a story by Jack London

He knew how to kill bears.

Winters are dark in the North Pole. When the storms come winds howl across the ice, the air is filled with snow, and no one ventures out. That is a good time to tell the story of Keesh—how Keesh, from the poorest igloo in the village, rose to power and became the leader of his people. This is his story.

Keesh lived in the North Pole a long time ago. He lived near the edge of the polar sea. He was a bright thirteen-year-old boy with a strong, healthy body. His father was a brave man who had died during a famine in the village. His father tried to save the lives of his people by fighting a giant polar bear. Keesh's father was crushed to death during the struggle. But he killed the bear, and the meat from the bear kept the people from starving.

Keesh was his only son, and he lived alone with his mother. But people are forgetful, and they soon forgot how Keesh's father had saved their lives. And since Keesh was only a boy and his mother was a woman and not a warrior, they were forced to live in the smallest and poorest igloo in the village.

One night there was a council meeting in the large igloo of Klosh-Kwan, who was the chief. Then Keesh showed how much courage he possessed. He rose to his feet and waited for silence. Then, with the dignity of an older man, he said, "It is true that my mother and I are given meat to eat. But the meat is always old and tough, filled with bones, and difficult to eat."

The hunters—both the young and the old—were shocked to hear a child speak to them that way.

But Keesh went on steadily. "Because my father, Bok, was a great hunter, I can speak these words. You know that Bok brought

home more meat than any hunter in the village. You know that he, himself, cut up the meat and shared it with everyone in the village. The oldest woman, the weakest old man, received a fair share."

"Quiet!" shouted the men. "Throw the child out! Send him to bed! No child may speak such words to warriors like us!"

Keesh waited calmly until the shouting died down.

"My mother has no one except me, and therefore I must speak. My father put his life in danger, and died, to provide food for this village. It is only right that I, his son, and Ikeega, who was his wife, should have enough good meat to eat as long as there is plenty of good meat in the village. I, Keesh, the son of Bok, have spoken."

He sat down.

He could hear angry murmuring all around him.

"It is not right for a boy to speak like that in this council," old Ugh-Gluk was muttering.

Massuk stood up. "Shall a child tell us how to act!" he demanded loudly. "I am a man! Must I listen to every child who cries for food?"

Some of the men began to shout at Keesh. They ordered him to leave. They threatened to punish him by not giving him any food at all.

Keesh's eyes flashed and the blood pounded under his skin. In the midst of the noise and the uproar, he jumped to his feet.

"Listen to me, you men!" he shouted. "I shall never speak in this council again—not until you come to me and say, 'Keesh, we want you to speak.'"

Keesh raised his arm and said, "My father, Bok, was a great hunter. I, his son, shall also go out and hunt the meat that I eat. When I return with meat, I will divide it fairly. No old person will cry out in hunger at night, while young warriors are holding their stomachs in pain because they have eaten too much. I, Keesh, have said this."

They laughed at Keesh and followed him out of the igloo, shouting at him. But Keesh said nothing more. He walked away with his head erect, looking neither to the left nor the right.

The next day Keesh went down to the shore where the ice and the land came together. Those who saw him go noticed that he carried his bow and a large supply of arrows. Across his shoulder was his father's big hunting spear.

There was laughter and much talk, for nothing like this had ever occurred before. Boys of his age did not go out to hunt, and they certainly never went out to hunt alone. People shook their heads gravely, and the women looked sadly at Ikeega, who was extremely worried about her son.

"He will be back before too long," said the women to cheer her up.

But the hunters said, "Let him go. This will teach him a lesson. He will return shortly. Then he will be quiet and meek and will know his place in the village."

But a day passed, and a second day, and on the third day there was a storm and wild gales blew and still there was no Keesh. Ikeega's face was filled with grief, and the women spoke bitterly to the men, saying that they had mistreated the boy and had sent him to his death. The men did not answer, and they prepared to search for the body when the storm was over.

Early the next morning, however, Keesh marched into the village. But he did not return in shame. Across his shoulders he carried some fresh-killed meat. And when he spoke, it was with authority and pride.

He said to the men, "Take some dogs and sleds and follow my path for a day. Eventually you will find much meat on the ice—a bear and her two cubs."

Ikeega was overjoyed, but Keesh said simply, "Come, Ikeega, let us eat. After that I shall sleep, for I am weary."

And he went into their igloo and ate a great deal, and then he slept for twenty hours.

At first there was much doubt and discussion. It is very dangerous to kill a polar bear, and it is three times as dangerous to

kill a mother bear with her cubs. The men could not believe that the boy Keesh, all by himself, had accomplished something so incredible. But the women pointed out that he had returned with fresh-killed meat on his back, and this was a powerful argument. So the men finally departed, grumbling, and saying that even if it were true, he had probably not cut up the carcasses[1] into pieces. In the North it is very important to do this as soon as the kill is made. If not, the meat freezes so solidly that it cannot be cut, and a three-hundred-pound bear, frozen stiff, is a very difficult thing to put on a sled and haul over bumpy ice. However, when they arrived at the spot, they found not only the kill, which they had doubted, but that Keesh had cut up the carcasses exactly the way a hunter should do it.

Thus began the mystery of Keesh. It was a mystery that deepened and grew with the passing of the days. On his very next trip Keesh killed a young bear, and on the following trip he killed two large bears. Usually he was gone for three to four days, although it was not

1. *carcass:* the body of a dead animal.

unusual for him to stay away for a week at a time. And Keesh always went alone, for he did not wish to have company on these trips.

The people were amazed. "How does he do it?" they asked one another. "He never even takes a dog with him, and dogs are such a great help too!"

"Why do you hunt only bears?" Klosh-Kwan asked him one day.

Keesh gave him a very good answer. "Everyone knows that there is more meat on the bear," he said.

But people in the village also talked about magic. "He must know magic," some of the men said. "Perhaps he hunts with evil spirits, and the evil spirits help him."

But other people said, "Maybe the spirits are not evil, but good. You know that his father was a mighty hunter. Is it possible that his father, somehow, helps him to hunt? It is hard to understand. Who knows?"

Still, his success continued, and the less skillful hunters were often kept busy hauling in his meat. Keesh shared the meat fairly. As his father had done, he made sure that the weakest old woman and the frailest old man received a fair share. As for himself, he never took more than he needed. Because of this and his ability as a hunter, Keesh was looked upon with great respect. There was talk about making him chief after old Klosh-Kwan died. They hoped that Keesh would come to the council again to speak, but he never did, and they were ashamed to ask him.

"I wish to build an igloo for myself," Keesh said one day to Klosh-Kwan and some of the hunters. "It should be a large igloo where Ikeega and I can dwell in comfort."

"Yes," they nodded.

"But I have no time. My business is hunting, and it takes all my time. So it is only right that the men and women of the village who eat my meat should build me my igloo."

The igloo that they built was very spacious. It was even larger than Klosh-Kwan's igloo. Keesh and his mother moved into it, and it was the first comfort she had enjoyed since the death of Bok. And because of her wonderful son, she came to be looked upon as the most important woman in the village, and the other women visited her to ask for advice and to be guided by her wisdom.

But it was the mystery of Keesh's marvelous hunting that was the main thing on everyone's mind. And one day Ugh-Gluk spoke to Keesh face-to-face.

"People say," said Ugh-Gluk, in an unfriendly way, "that you have some magic power, that evil spirits help you when you are hunting."

Keesh answered him by saying, "Isn't the meat good? Has anyone in the

village ever become sick by eating it? How do you know that magic or evil spirits are involved—or do you say that because you are so envious of me?"

And Ugh-Gluk went away feeling very embarrassed.

But in the council one night, they discussed Keesh for a long time. Finally, they decided to spy on him when he went out to hunt, so that they could learn his methods. On his next trip, two clever young hunters, Bim and Bawn, followed Keesh. They stayed a good distance behind him and made sure that he did not see them. They kept an eye on him and on everything he did.

Five days later they returned, eager to tell what they had seen. The council was hastily called and Bim began to speak. He said, "Fellow warriors, as you ordered, we followed Keesh. We followed him very slyly, so that he was not aware we were behind him. In the middle of the first day, he saw a large bear. It was a *very* large bear."

"I have never seen a bigger one," said Bawn.

"But the bear did not wish to fight," said Bim, "for the bear turned away from Keesh and went off in the other direction over the ice. We saw this as we watched from the rocks near the shore. Then the bear came our way and Keesh ran after him, completely unafraid. Keesh shouted loudly at the bear, waved his arms around, and continued to yell. Then, finally, the bear got angry, rose up on his hind legs, and began to growl. But Keesh walked right up to the bear."

"Yes," said Bawn, continuing the story. "Keesh walked right up to the bear. The bear began to chase him and Keesh ran away. But as Keesh ran, he dropped a little round ball on the ice. The bear stopped and smelled it, then swallowed it. Keesh continued to run away and drop little round balls, and the bear continued to swallow them all."

There were cries of doubt, and Ugh-Gluk said that he did not believe it.

"We saw it with our own eyes!" Bawn exclaimed.

"Yes," said Bim, "we saw it with our own eyes. This continued, and then the bear suddenly stood upright and roared loudly in pain and ran around wildly, beating its paws madly against its body. Keesh ran a safe distance away, but the bear ignored him, since it was concerned only with the terrible pain the little round balls had caused inside him."

"Yes," Bawn interrupted him. "It was a pain inside him because he clawed at himself and growled and squealed and jumped frantically around. I never saw such a sight!"

"Never!" said Bim. "And furthermore, it was a very large bear."

"Perhaps it was some kind of magic," Ugh-Gluk suggested.

"I do not know," Bim replied. "I can only tell you what I saw with my eyes. After a while the bear grew weak and tired, for he was very heavy and had been jumping around violently. Finally he went off to the ice along the shore, shaking his head slowly from side to side, and sitting down now and then to squeal and cry. Keesh followed the bear, and we followed Keesh. For three more days we followed them. The bear grew weaker and weaker and never ceased crying from its pain."

"It was magic!" Ugh-Gluk exclaimed. "Surely it was magic!"

"It may well be."

Bim went on, "The bear wandered back and forth, back and forth, going in circles, so that, at the end, he was near the place where Keesh had first seen him. By this time the bear was very sick and was not able to crawl any further, so Keesh came up close to him and speared him to death."

"And then?" Klosh-Kwan demanded.

"Then we left Keesh skinning the bear and came running back to tell you what we had seen."

That afternoon the women hauled in the meat of the bear while the men sat in council. When Keesh arrived, a messenger was sent to him asking him to come to the council. But he sent a reply saying that he was hungry and tired, and also that his igloo was large and comfortable and could hold many men.

The whole council was so curious that all of the men got up and went to Keesh's igloo at once. Keesh was eating, but he greeted them with respect.

Klosh-Kwan repeated the information that had been brought by Bim and Bawn. When he had finished he said in a stern voice, "So we need an explanation, Keesh, of the way you hunt. Is there magic in it?"

Keesh looked up and smiled. "No, Klosh-Kwan, how would a boy know anything about magic? I know nothing about that. But I have figured out a way to kill bears easily. I use my mind and not magic. That is all."

"And may any man kill bears that way?"

"Yes, any man."

There was a long silence. The men looked at each other, and Keesh went on eating.

"And . . . and . . . and will you tell us, Keesh?" Klosh-Kwan finally asked in a trembling voice.

"Yes, I will tell you." Keesh rose to his feet. "It is quite simple. Watch!"

He picked up a thin piece of whalebone and showed it to them. The ends of the bone were as sharp as a knife. He bent the piece in half in his hand. When he released it, it sprang back, straight. Keesh picked up a piece of whale meat.

"So," he said, "I take a small piece of whale meat like this and make it hollow. Into the hollow I put the sharp whalebone, bent tightly in half. I force another piece of meat into the hollow. After that I put it outside where it freezes into a little round ball. The bear swallows the ball, the meat melts, and the whalebone springs back with its sharp edges standing out straight. After a while the bear gets sick, and when the bear is very sick, why you kill him with a spear. It is quite simple."

Ugh-Gluk said, "Oh!" and Klosh-Kwan said, "Ah!" And everyone understood.

This is the story of Keesh who lived long ago by the edge of the polar sea. Because he used his brain, he rose to power and became the chief of his village. And through all the years that he lived, his people had enough to eat, and no one who was weak or old ever cried aloud at night because there was no meat.

YOU CAN ANSWER THESE QUESTIONS

Put an *x* in the box next to the correct answer.

Reading Comprehension

1. Keesh's father was killed by
   - ❏ **a.** another warrior.
   - ❏ **b.** hungry wolves.
   - ❏ **c.** a bear.

2. When Keesh complained at a council meeting, the hunters were
   - ❏ **a.** pleased.
   - ❏ **b.** amused.
   - ❏ **c.** shocked.

3. What did Keesh do with the meat from the bears he killed?
   - ❏ **a.** He kept all of it.
   - ❏ **b.** He gave most of it to his mother.
   - ❏ **c.** He shared it fairly with everyone.

4. Bim and Bawn followed Keesh to
   - ❏ **a.** discover how he killed the bears.
   - ❏ **b.** help him hunt.
   - ❏ **c.** make sure that he was safe.

5. The bear became sick after it
   - ❏ **a.** ate the little round pieces of meat.
   - ❏ **b.** fell and hurt its paw.
   - ❏ **c.** was attacked by Bim and Bawn.

6. Which statement is true?
   - ❏ **a.** Keesh killed the bears by using magic.
   - ❏ **b.** Keesh became the chief.
   - ❏ **c.** Keesh never explained how he killed the bears.

Vocabulary

7. It was incredible that a boy could kill three bears. The word *incredible* means
   - ❏ **a.** hard to believe.
   - ❏ **b.** easy to understand.
   - ❏ **c.** not very interesting.

8. The bear roared in pain and jumped around frantically. The word *frantically* means
   - ❏ **a.** gladly.
   - ❏ **b.** wildly.
   - ❏ **c.** slowly.

Idioms

9. Keesh waited calmly until the shouting died down. The idiom *to die down* means
   - ❏ **a.** to hurt someone.
   - ❏ **b.** to get louder.
   - ❏ **c.** to slowly end.

10. Bim and Bawn kept an eye on Keesh. The idiom *to keep an eye on* means
    - ❏ **a.** to watch.
    - ❏ **b.** to warn.
    - ❏ **c.** to worry about.

How many questions did you answer correctly? Circle your score. Then fill in your score on the Score Chart on page 184.

Number Correct	1	2	3	4	5	6	7	8	9	10
Score	10	20	30	40	50	60	70	80	90	100

Exercise A

Understanding the story. Answer each question with a complete sentence. You may look back at the story.

1. Where did Keesh live?

   _____

2. How did Keesh's father die?

   _____

3. What did Bok do with the meat he brought back?

   _____

4. How many bears did Keesh kill the first time he went hunting?

   _____

5. What did the council order Bim and Bawn to do?

   _____

   _____

6. What did Keesh drop on the ice for the bear to eat?

   _____

   _____

7. Did Keesh use magic or his mind to kill the bears?

   _____

8. What did Keesh put into each piece of whale meat?

   _____

   _____

Exercise B

Adding vocabulary. On the left are 8 words from the story. Complete each sentence by adding the correct word.

meek

igloo

murmuring

ventures

erect

mistreated

famine

uproar

1. Keesh and his mother lived in the poorest

   _____ in the village.

2. When the storms come and the air is filled with

   snow, no one _____ out.

3. During the _____, there was not

   enough food for the people of the village.

4. Keesh could hear voices _____

   all around him.

5. The men believed that a boy should be quiet

   and _____.

6. There was an _____ when the

   warriors began to shout.

7. Keesh walked away with his head

   _____, looking neither to the

   left nor the right.

8. The women thought that the men had

   _____ the boy and had sent him

   to his death.

Exercise C

Adding punctuation. The following direct quotations need **punctuation marks**. Add capital letters, quotation marks, commas, periods, question marks, and exclamation points as needed. Write the corrected sentences on the lines. The first one has been done for you.

1. Keesh said you know that my father was a great hunter

   Keesh said, "You know that my father was a great hunter."

2. Keesh told the warriors i will go out and hunt for food

   _____

   _____

3. a man angrily yelled throw the child out

   _____

   _____

4. Ikeega asked has Keesh returned yet

   _____

5. he will be back soon the women answered

   _____

   _____

6. Keesh said i shall sleep for i am weary

   _____

   _____

7. how does Keesh kill the bears the men asked one another

_____

_____

8. a warrior asked why do you hunt only bears

_____

_____

9. Bim said we saw the bear sit down and cry

_____

_____

10. Bawn exclaimed i never saw such a sight

_____

_____

Exercise D

Finding synonyms. Read each sentence. Then select the **synonym** (the word most similar in meaning) for the word in capital letters. Circle the letter of the correct answer. Each capitalized word appears in the story.

1. Keesh's father was crushed to death during a struggle with a bear.

   STRUGGLE   **a.** fight   **b.** meal   **c.** trip

2. Everyone was surprised since nothing like that had ever occurred before.

   OCCURRED   **a.** needed   **b.** wanted   **c.** happened

3. On the third day there was a storm, and wild gales blew.

   GALES   **a.** winds   **b.** snow   **c.** rain

4. The men did not want to go out, so they departed, grumbling.

   GRUMBLING   **a.** smiling   **b.** complaining   **c.** rushing

5. Some of the hunters were hauling in the meat from the bear.

   HAULING   **a.** pulling   **b.** eating   **c.** cutting

6. Keesh lived in the best igloo in the village; it was very spacious.

   SPACIOUS   **a.** small   **b.** large   **c.** weak

7. Keesh thought that Ugh-Gluk was envious because Keesh was a much better hunter.

   ENVIOUS   **a.** jealous   **b.** tired   **c.** glad

8. The bear kept getting weaker and never ceased crying from the pain.

   CEASED   **a.** tried   **b.** stopped   **c.** started

Exercise E

Part A

Building sentences by using connectives. Connectives are words that connect sentences smoothly and clearly. Usually, connectives appear at the beginning of a sentence, followed by a comma. Some common connectives are *however, therefore, finally, furthermore,* and *thus.* Become familiar with these connectives. You will find them to be very useful in your writing.

Below are 10 pairs of sentences. Begin the second sentence in each pair with the **connective** in parentheses. Use capital letters and commas. Write both sentences on the lines. The first one has been done for you.

1. Storms are very dangerous in the North Pole. No one goes out during storms. (therefore)

   Storms are very dangerous in the North Pole.
   Therefore, no one goes out during storms.

2. Keesh's father, Bok, was killed by a bear. Bok killed the bear in the struggle. (however)

   _____

   _____

   _____

   _____

3. The warriors were very angry with Keesh. They asked him to leave. (therefore)

   _____

   _____

   _____

   _____

4. Keesh was gone for a long time. He returned with some meat. (finally)

_____

_____

_____

5. Keesh killed more bears than anyone. He always shared the meat fairly. (furthermore)

_____

_____

_____

6. For a long time the warriors wondered how Keesh killed the bears. They sent two young men to follow him. (finally)

_____

_____

_____

7. Keesh was too busy to build an igloo. The people of the village built one for him. (thus)

_____

_____

_____

_____

8. Keesh saw a very large bear. The bear did not wish to fight. (however)

_____

_____

_____

_____

9. No one could understand how Keesh killed the bears. People thought he had some magic powers. (thus)

_____

_____

_____

_____

10. The people of the village respected Keesh very much. He eventually became their chief. (therefore)

_____

_____

_____

_____

Part B

A **topic sentence** gives the **main idea** of a **paragraph.** Below are 3 topic sentences. Add a sentence to each. Begin the sentence with the connective that has been provided.

1. Keesh thought that he and his mother were not receiving their fair share of good meat. Therefore,

   _____

   _____

   _____

   _____

2. Keesh was the best hunter in the village. For example,

   _____

   _____

   _____

   _____

3. The men wanted to know how Keesh killed the bears. Thus,

   _____

   _____

   _____

   _____

Select one of the three topics from page 40. Write the two sentences on the lines below, and then complete the paragraph.

_____

_____

_____

_____

_____

_____

_____

_____

_____

_____

_____

_____

_____

_____

You have now written a **paragraph** with a **topic sentence**.

Exercise F
Vocabulary review. Write a complete sentence for each word or group of words.

1. incredible _____

_____

2. frantically _____

_____

3. meek _____

_____

4. famine _____

_____

5. murmuring _____

_____

6. gales _____

_____

7. spacious _____

_____

8. mistreated _____

_____

9. to die down _____

_____

10. keep an eye on _____

_____

Sharing with Others

This section provides you with opportunities to share your thoughts and ideas with others, while you practice and improve your reading, writing, speaking, and listening skills.

Part A

Discuss the following questions. Share your answers with your partner or with the group.

1. Do you think it was right for the boy, Keesh, to complain to the council? Why? Does the fact that Keesh's father was a great hunter make a difference? Explain.

2. Should the men have shouted at Keesh and asked him to leave? Is there some other way they might have handled the situation?

3. Show that Keesh's father set an excellent example for his son.

4. The author stated, "People are forgetful, and they soon forgot how Keesh's father had saved their lives." Do you think that most people quickly forget the good deeds of others? If you wish, use one or two personal examples to support your opinion.

5. Why did the villagers think that Keesh had magical powers?

6. Keesh thought of an excellent way to kill bears. Still, his method was dangerous and required him to be a very fine hunter. Present facts to support this statement.

7. If you were Keesh, would you have revealed how you killed the bears— or would you have tried to hide your secret? Why?

Part B

1. Write a **paragraph** to answer Question 7. Start the paragraph with a **topic sentence.** Then give reasons to support your point of view. Begin the last sentence of the paragraph with *therefore* or *thus*.

_____

_____

_____

_____

_____

_____

_____

_____

_____

_____

_____

_____

_____

_____

_____

_____

_____

2. On the lines below, **summarize** what Bim and Bawn told the council. You may look back at the story.

_____

_____

_____

_____

_____

_____

_____

_____

_____

_____

_____

_____

_____

_____

_____

_____

_____

THE FORCE OF LUCK

based on a story by Rudolfo A. Anaya
and José Griego y Maestas

Before You Read

Connections

Study the picture on the left. Describe what you see.

- What thing is the bird holding in its feet? Where else do you see this thing?
- What do you think is in the pouch?
- Why do you think the man is waving his arms and shouting?
- Do you think you will like this story? Why or why not?

As you read, think about how the picture connects to the story.

Words to Learn

In this story, you will learn some new words. You will also learn some *idioms*. For example, *it stands to reason* is an idiom that means "it is clear."

THE FORCE OF LUCK

based on a story by Rudolfo A. Anaya
and José Griego y Maestas

The stories he told were hard to believe.

Once two wealthy friends got into a lively argument. One said that to become rich a man needed to start with some money. The other said that to become rich all a man needed was luck. They argued for a long time. Finally, they decided that if they could find an honorable man, he might be able to prove who was right.

One day while they were traveling through a small village, they noticed a miller[1] who was grinding corn and wheat. They paused and asked the man about his work. The miller told them that he worked for a boss and that he earned only fifty cents a day, with which he had to support a family of five.

The friends were surprised. "Are you saying that you can support a family of five on only fifteen dollars a month?" one man asked.

"I live modestly to make ends meet," the humble miller replied.

The two friends spoke privately and agreed that this man might be able to help them resolve their argument.

"I am going to make you an offer," one of them said to the miller. "I will give you two hundred dollars and you may do whatever you want with the money."

"But why would you give me that money when you've just met me?" the miller asked.

One man explained. "My friend and I have been arguing about something for a long time. He says that to become rich all a man needs is luck. I say that to become rich a man needs to start with a

1. *miller:* a person who runs a mill. A mill grinds grain into flour.

good amount of money. By giving you this money, perhaps we can settle our argument. Here, take it, and do whatever you want with it."

So the miller took the money and spent the rest of the day thinking about the strange meeting during which he had received more money than he had ever seen.

When the day's work was done, the miller decided the first thing he would do would be to buy food for his family. He took out ten dollars and wrapped the rest of the money in a piece of cloth and put the bundle of money in his bag. Then he went to the market and bought supplies and a piece of meat to take home for dinner.

On the way home he was attacked by a hawk that had smelled the meat which the miller was carrying. The miller fought off the bird, but in the struggle the miller dropped the bag. Before the miller knew what was happening, the hawk grabbed the bag with the bundle of money and flew off with it.

"Ah," moaned the miller, "I should have let that hungry bird have the meat. I could have bought a lot more meat with the money he took. Unfortunately, now I'm as poor as I was before. And worse, because now those two men will say I am a thief!"

The miller gathered his supplies, continued on his way home, and told his wife the entire story when he arrived.

When he was finished telling his story, his wife said, "We have always been poor, but perhaps someday our luck will change."

The next day the miller went to work as usual, and before long he forgot the entire matter.

Three months after he had lost the money to the hawk, the two wealthy men returned to the village. As soon as they saw the miller, they approached him and asked him if his luck had changed. When the miller saw them, he felt ashamed and was afraid they would think that he had squandered the money on worthless things. But he decided to tell them the truth, and so he told them the story. The men believed him. In fact, the one who insisted that it was money and not luck that made a man prosper took out another two hundred dollars and gave it to the miller.

"Let's try again," he said, "and let's see what happens this time."

The miller didn't know what to think. He said, "You are very kind, but maybe it would be better if you gave this money to another man."

"No," the man insisted. "I want to give it to you because you are an honest man, and if we are going to settle our argument, you have to take the money!"

The miller thanked them and promised to do his best. Then as soon as the two men left, he began to think about what to do with the money so that it wouldn't disappear again. The thing to do was to take the money straight home. He took out ten dollars, wrapped the rest in a cloth, and immediately headed home.

When he arrived, his wife wasn't in the house. At first he didn't know what to do with the money. He went to the pantry where he kept a large clay jar filled with grain. That was as safe a place as any to hide the money, he thought, so he emptied out the grain and put the bundle of money at the bottom of the jar. Then he covered the money with the grain so that it was hidden. Satisfied that the money was safe, he returned to work.

That afternoon when he arrived home from work, he was greeted by his wife.

"Look," she said, very pleased, "today I bought some paint to paint the house."

"And how did you buy paint since we don't have any money?" he asked.

"Well, the man who was selling the paint was willing to trade for jewelry, money, or anything of value," she said. "The only thing we had of value was the jar full of grain, so I traded it for the paint. Isn't it wonderful? I think we have enough paint to paint these two rooms!"

"What have you done?" groaned the man. "We're ruined again!"

"But why?" she asked, unable to understand his anguish.

"Today I met the same two friends who gave me the two hundred dollars three months ago," he explained. "After I told them how I lost the money, they gave me another two hundred dollars. To make sure that the money was safe, I came home and hid it inside the jar filled with grain—the same jar you traded for paint! Now we're as poor as we were before! What am I going to tell the two men? They'll think I'm a liar and a thief, for sure!"

"Let them think what they want," his wife said calmly. "If it is our destiny to be poor, then we will be poor. Tell them the truth. That is all you can do."

These words consoled the miller, and the next day he went to work as usual. Time passed, and one day the two wealthy friends returned to ask the miller how he had done with the second two hundred dollars. When the miller saw them, he was afraid they would accuse him of being a liar and a spendthrift, but he was truthful and told them what had happened to the money.

"I find your stories hard to believe," said one of the men. "I think you lost the money gambling, and that's why you're telling us these wild stories. Anyway," he continued, "I still believe that it is money and not luck that makes a man prosper."

"Well, you certainly didn't prove your point by giving the money to this poor miller," his friend reminded him. "Good day, you unlucky man," he said to the miller.

"Thank you, friends," the miller said.

"Oh, by the way," said the man who believed in luck, "here is a piece of lead I've been carrying around. It is worthless to me, but maybe you can use it for something." Then the two men left, still debating their different points of view.

Since the piece of lead was hardly worth anything, the miller thought nothing of it and put it in his jacket pocket. By the time he arrived home, he had forgotten about it. Later that night after the family had eaten and gone to bed, they heard a knock at the door.

"Who is it? What do you want?" the miller asked.

"It's me, your neighbor," a voice answered. The miller recognized the fisherman's voice. "I've come to ask you if you have any lead you can spare. I'm going fishing tomorrow and I need the lead to weigh down the nets."

The miller remembered the lead, got up, found it, and gave it to the fisherman.

"Thank you very much, neighbor," he said. "I promise you the first fish I catch tomorrow will be yours."

"Think nothing of it," the miller said and returned to bed. The next day he got up and went to work without thinking about the incident. But in the afternoon when he returned home, he found his wife cooking a big fish for dinner.

"Since when are we so well off we can afford fish for supper?" he asked his wife.

"Don't you remember that our neighbor promised us the first fish he caught?" his wife reminded him. "Well, this was the first fish he

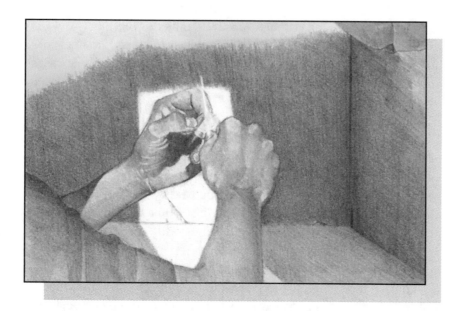

caught. So it's ours, and it's a beauty. But you should have been here when I cut it open. I found a large piece of glass in its stomach!"

"And what did you do with it?"

"Oh, I gave it to the children to play with," she shrugged.

When the miller saw the piece of glass, he noticed it shone so brightly it appeared to illuminate the room, but since he knew nothing about jewels, he didn't realize that it was valuable, and he left it with the children. But the bright glass was so attractive that the children were soon fighting over it and making a terrible noise.

Now it happened that the miller and his wife had other neighbors who were jewelers. The following morning, after the miller had left for work, the jeweler's wife visited the miller's wife to complain about all the noise her children had made.

"I know, and I'm sorry, but you know how it is with children," the miller's wife explained. "Yesterday we found a beautiful piece of glass, and I gave it to my youngest child to play with, and when the others tried to take it away from him, he raised a storm."

The jeweler's wife became very interested. "Will you show me that piece of glass?" she asked.

"Of course. Here it is."

"Ah, yes, it's a pretty piece of glass. Where did you find it?"

"Our neighbor gave us a fish yesterday, and when I was cleaning it, I found the glass in its stomach."

"Why don't you let me take it home for just a moment. You see, I have one just like it, and I want to compare them."

"Yes, why not? Take it," answered the miller's wife.

So the jeweler's wife ran off with the glass to show it to her husband. When the jeweler saw the glass, he instantly knew it was one of the finest diamonds he had ever seen.

"It's a diamond!" he exclaimed.

"I thought so," his wife nodded eagerly. "What shall we do?"

"Go tell the neighbor we'll give her fifty dollars for it, but don't tell her it's a diamond!"

"No, no," his wife chuckled, "of course not." She ran to her neighbor's house. "Ah, yes, we have one exactly like this," she told the miller's wife. "My husband is willing to buy it for fifty dollars—just so that we can have a pair, you understand."

"I can't sell it," the miller's wife answered. "You will have to wait until my husband returns from work."

That evening when the miller came home from work, his wife told him about the offer the jeweler had made for the piece of glass.

"But why would they offer fifty dollars for a worthless piece of glass?" the miller wondered aloud. Before his wife could answer they were interrupted by the jeweler's wife.

"What do you say, neighbor, will you take fifty dollars for the glass?" she asked.

"No, that's not enough," the miller said cautiously. "Offer more."

"I'll give you fifty thousand!" the jeweler's wife blurted out.

"A little bit more," the miller replied.

"Impossible!" the jeweler's wife cried, "I can't offer any more without consulting my husband." She ran off to tell her husband how the bargaining was going, and he told her he was prepared to pay a hundred thousand dollars to acquire the diamond.

He handed her seventy-five thousand dollars and said, "Take this and tell him that tomorrow, as soon as I open my shop, he'll have the rest."

When the miller heard the offer and saw the money, he couldn't believe his eyes. He thought that the jeweler's wife was jesting with him. But it was a genuine offer, and he received a hundred thousand dollars for the diamond.

The miller had never seen so much money, and all morning he thought about what he might do with it. That afternoon his wife asked him what he had decided to do with their new fortune.

"I think I will start my own mill," he answered. "It will be like the one I operate now. Once I set up my business, we'll see how our luck changes."

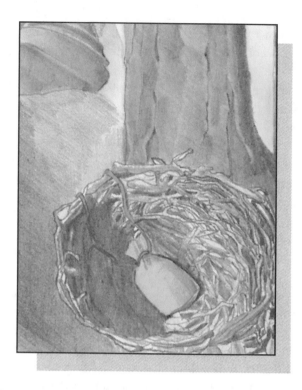

The next day he proceeded to buy everything he needed to establish his mill and to build a new house. Soon he had everything going.

Six months passed since he had seen the two men who had given him the four hundred dollars and the piece of lead. He was eager to see them again and to tell them how the piece of lead had changed his luck and made him wealthy.

Time passed and the miller prospered. His business grew and grew, and he even built a summer home where he could take his family on vacation. He had many employees who worked for him. One day while he was at his store, he saw the two men riding by. He rushed out into the street to greet them and asked them to come in. He was overjoyed to see them, and he was happy to see that they admired his store.

"Tell us the truth," the man who had given him the four hundred dollars said. "You used that money to set up this business."

The miller swore he hadn't, and he told them how he had given the piece of lead to his neighbor and how the fisherman had, in return, given him a fish with a very large diamond in its stomach. And he told them how he had sold the diamond.

"That's how I was able to acquire this business," he said. "But it's time to eat. Let's eat, and then I'll show you everything I have now."

The men agreed, but one of them still doubted the miller's story. So they ate and then the three men rode out to see the miller's summer house. The house was on the other side of the river where the mountains were cool and beautiful. When they arrived, the men admired the place very much. It was such a peaceful place that they rode all afternoon through the forest. During their ride, they passed by a tall pine tree.

"What is that on top of the tree?" one of them asked.

"That's a hawk's nest," the miller replied.

"I have never seen one. I would like to take a closer look at the nest."

"Of course," the miller said, and he ordered a servant to climb up the tree and bring down the nest so that his friend could see how it was made. When the hawk's nest was on the ground, they examined it carefully. They noticed that there was a cloth bag at the bottom of the nest. When the miller saw the bag, he immediately realized that it was the same bag he had lost to the hawk that fought him for the piece of meat years ago.

"You won't believe me, friends," he told them, "but I put almost all of the first two hundred dollars you gave me into this bag."

"If it's the same bag," said the man who had doubted him, "then it stands to reason that the money the hawk took should be in the bag."

"There's no doubt about that," the miller said. "Let's see what we find."

The three of them examined the old, weather-beaten bag, and although it was full of holes, when they ripped it apart they found that the money was there. The two men remembered what the miller had told them, and they agreed that he was an honest man. Still, the man who had given him the money wasn't satisfied. He wondered what had really happened to the second two hundred dollars he had given the miller.

They spent the rest of the day riding in the mountains and returned to the house very late.

The servant in charge of feeding the horses suddenly realized that he had no grain for them. He ran to the barn and checked, but there was no grain for the hungry horses. So he ran to a neighbor and bought from him a large clay jar that was filled with grain. He carried the jar home and emptied the grain into a bucket to feed it to the horses. When he got to the bottom of the jar, he noticed a bulge that turned out to be something wrapped in a piece of cloth. He immediately went inside.

"Master," he said, "look at this package that I found in a jar of grain which I just bought from our neighbor!"

The three men carefully unwrapped the cloth and found the other one hundred ninety dollars that the miller had told them he had lost. That is how the miller proved to his friends that he was truly an honest man.

And they had to decide for themselves whether it had been luck or money that had made the miller a wealthy man!

YOU CAN ANSWER THESE QUESTIONS

Put an *x* in the box next to the correct answer.

Reading Comprehension

1. The miller said that he earned
   - ❏ **a.** fifty cents a day.
   - ❏ **b.** five dollars a day.
   - ❏ **c.** fifteen dollars a day.

2. At their first meeting, the men gave the miller
   - ❏ **a.** exactly fifty dollars.
   - ❏ **b.** nearly one hundred dollars.
   - ❏ **c.** two hundred dollars.

3. What happened to the bag with the money?
   - ❏ **a.** The miller lost it at the market.
   - ❏ **b.** A bird flew away with it.
   - ❏ **c.** Some neighbors stole it.

4. Later, the miller hid some money
   - ❏ **a.** in his garden.
   - ❏ **b.** under his bed.
   - ❏ **c.** in a jar filled with grain.

5. How did the miller and his wife get the diamond?
   - ❏ **a.** The miller's wife found it in a fish.
   - ❏ **b.** The miller bought it from a neighbor.
   - ❏ **c.** It was given to them by two wealthy men.

6. What did the men find in the hawk's nest?
   - ❏ **a.** some eggs
   - ❏ **b.** a bag filled with money
   - ❏ **c.** a piece of glass

Vocabulary

7. The miller hadn't squandered the money on foolish things. The word *squandered* means
   - ❏ **a.** wasted.
   - ❏ **b.** wanted.
   - ❏ **c.** received.

8. The glass shone so brightly, it was able to illuminate the room. The word *illuminate* means
   - ❏ **a.** fix or repair.
   - ❏ **b.** light up.
   - ❏ **c.** make dark.

9. The miller bought everything he needed to establish his own mill. The word *establish* means
   - ❏ **a.** look after or watch.
   - ❏ **b.** set up or start.
   - ❏ **c.** go away from or leave.

Idioms

10. It stands to reason that the money should be in the bag. The idiom *it stands to reason* means
    - ❏ **a.** it is clear.
    - ❏ **b.** it is wrong.
    - ❏ **c.** it is strange.

How many questions did you answer correctly? Circle your score. Then fill in your score on the Score Chart on page 184.

Number Correct	1	2	3	4	5	6	7	8	9	10
Score	10	20	30	40	50	60	70	80	90	100

Exercise A

Understanding the story. Answer each question with a complete sentence. You may look back at the story.

1. When the men met the miller, how much money did they give him?

   _____

   _____

2. How did the miller lose the bag of money?

   _____

   _____

3. How much money did the men give the miller when they saw him again?

   _____

   _____

4. How did the miller hide the money?

   _____

   _____

5. How did the miller's wife get paint for the house?

   _____

   _____

6. What did the miller give the fisherman?

   _____

   _____

7. What did the miller's wife find inside the fish?

_____

_____

8. How much money did the miller receive for the diamond?

_____

_____

9. What did the men see at the bottom of the hawk's nest?

_____

_____

10. When the men unwrapped the cloth, how much money did they find?

_____

_____

Exercise B

Adding vocabulary. On the left are 10 words from the story. Complete each sentence by adding the correct word.

acquire

consoled

honorable

employees

insisted

spendthrift

blurted

destiny

jesting

consulting

1. Two men were looking for someone they could trust. They were seeking an _____ man.

2. The miller wanted to return the money, but the men _____ that he keep it.

3. The miller was afraid the men would think that he was a _____ who had wasted the money.

4. The miller's wife said, "If it is our _____ to be poor, then we will be poor."

5. After he spoke to his wife, the miller felt better; her words _____ him.

6. "I'll give you fifty thousand dollars!" the jeweler's wife suddenly _____ out.

7. The jeweler's wife couldn't offer any more money without _____ her husband.

8. The miller thought the jeweler's wife was joking, or _____, with him.

9. With the money he received for the diamond, the miller was able to _____ a business.

10. After the miller became wealthy, he hired many _____ who worked in his business.

Exercise C

Part A

Putting events in order. Put the events in the order in which they occurred. You may look back at the story. The first one has been done for you.

1. _b_   **a.** The miller's wife traded the jar of grain for some paint.

2. ____   **b.** Two friends met a miller and gave him two hundred dollars.

3. ____   **c.** The miller gave the lead to a fisherman.

4. ____   **d.** As the miller was going home, a hawk grabbed the bag with the money and flew away.

5. ____   **e.** The men gave the miller another two hundred dollars.

6. ____   **f.** The miller hid the money at the bottom of a jar filled with grain.

7. ____   **g.** The miller's wife found something shiny in the fish.

8. ____   **h.** The miller used the money to set up a business.

9. ____   **i.** The miller received a hundred thousand dollars.

10. ____   **j.** The men found the money in a jar filled with grain.

11. ____   **k.** The men found the money in a hawk's nest.

12. ____   **l.** One of the men gave the miller a piece of lead.

Part B

Now list the correct order of events on the lines below. The first one has been done for you.

1. _Two friends met a miller and gave him two hundred dollars._

2. _____

_____

3. _____

_____

4. _____

_____

5. _____

_____

6. _____

_____

7. _____

_____

8. _____

_____

9. _____

_____

10. _____

_____

11. _____

_____

12. _____

_____

Exercise D

Finding synonyms. Read each sentence. Then select the **synonym** (the word most similar in meaning) for the word in capital letters. Circle the letter of the correct answer. Each capitalized word appears in the story.

1. The two friends thought that the miller could help them resolve their argument.

   RESOLVE   **a.** settle   **b.** start   **c.** shout

2. The miller wrapped the money in a piece of cloth and put the bundle in his bag.

   BUNDLE   **a.** newspaper   **b.** package   **c.** box

3. When he realized his wife had given the money away, he was filled with anguish.

   ANGUISH   **a.** pleasure   **b.** power   **c.** pain

4. When the jeweler saw the piece of glass, he instantly knew it was a very fine diamond.

   INSTANTLY   **a.** immediately   **b.** never   **c.** later

5. They said that they would give him a hundred thousand dollars, and when he received the money, he knew that it was a genuine offer.

   GENUINE   **a.** false   **b.** true   **c.** foolish

6. The miller was overjoyed to see the men again, and he happily told them about his wealth.

   OVERJOYED   **a.** frightened   **b.** sorry   **c.** delighted

7. When the miller left the two men, they were still debating their different points of view.

   DEBATING   **a.** arguing   **b.** agreeing   **c.** asking

Exercise E

Part A

Building sentences. Combine two **simple sentences** into one **complex sentence** by using the **subordinating conjunction** in parentheses. Put the conjunction in the middle of the sentence. Then write the complex sentence on the line. The first one has been done for you.

Common Subordinating Conjunctions

after	since	although	so that
because	until	if	while

1. Two friends met a miller. They were traveling in a town. (while)

   Two friends met a miller while they were traveling in a town.

2. They gave the miller some money. He was an honest man. (since)

   _____

   _____

   _____

3. The hawk attacked the miller. The bird smelled the meat. (because)

   _____

   _____

   _____

4. The miller put the money in a jar. It was safe. (so that)

   _____

   _____

   _____

5. He covered the money with the grain. It was completely hidden. (until)

_____

_____

_____

6. She couldn't buy paint. She didn't have any money. (if)

_____

_____

_____

7. The miller didn't see the men for a long time. They rode away. (after)

_____

_____

_____

8. The miller was telling the truth. His story was strange. (, although)

_____

_____

_____

Part B

Combine the **simple sentences** into **complex sentences** by using the **subordinating conjunctions** below.

after   **until**   **because**   **so that**

Put the conjunctions in the middle of the sentence. Then write the sentence on the line. Use each conjunction once.

9. The men could give the miller money. They were wealthy.

_____

_____

_____

10. The servant climbed up the tree and brought down the nest. The man could see how it was made.

_____

_____

_____

11. The miller bought his own mill. He sold the diamond.

_____

_____

_____

12. They rode through the mountains. It was time to return to the miller's house.

_____

_____

_____

Exercise F

Vocabulary review. Write a complete sentence for each word or group of words.

1. illuminate _____

   _____

2. establish _____

   _____

3. acquire _____

   _____

4. jesting _____

   _____

5. employees _____

   _____

6. squandered _____

   _____

7. genuine _____

   _____

8. debating _____

   _____

9. overjoyed _____

   _____

10. it stands to reason _____

   _____

SHARING WITH OTHERS

This section provides you with opportunities to share your thoughts and ideas with others, while you practice and improve your reading, writing, speaking, and listening skills.

Part A

Discuss the following questions. Share your answers with your partner or with the group.

1. Explain why the two wealthy men were looking for someone they could trust.

2. Suppose that the miller's wife had not given the money away. Do you think the story would have had a different ending? Why?

3. Animals often play an important part in folktales. Show that this is true in "The Force of Luck."

4. Perhaps the miller was lucky. But he was also hardworking, honest, and wise. Explain how each of these virtues helped make the miller successful.

5. Luckily, the miller received a piece of lead. As a result of that, he found a diamond, which he sold for a hundred thousand dollars. Therefore, was it luck or money that led to the miller's success? Explain your answer.

6. Some people are superstitious. They believe it is "bad luck" to walk under a ladder or to break a mirror. Are you superstitious? If so, what do you try to avoid? What brings you "good luck"?

7. It is often said that "One makes one's luck." What does this mean? Do you agree?

8. Which would you rather have—money or luck? Explain.

9. What lesson or lessons does the story teach?

Part B

1. During the story, the miller was both lucky and unlucky. For example, the miller was lucky that the men gave him the money. But the miller was unlucky that the hawk took the money. Fill in the chart below. List all the times when the miller was lucky and unlucky. You will probably want to look back at the story.

Times when the miller was lucky

1. _____

_____

_____

_____

_____

_____

_____

_____

_____

_____

_____

_____

_____

_____

_____

Times when the miller was unlucky

1. _____

_____

_____

_____

_____

_____

_____

_____

_____

_____

_____

_____

_____

_____

_____

2. Write about a time when you were lucky or unlucky. If you write
about a lucky experience, use the title "Lucky Me." If you write about
an unlucky experience, use the title "Just My Luck."

_____

_____

_____

_____

_____

_____

_____

_____

_____

_____

_____

_____

_____

_____

_____

_____

_____

_____

_____

SIXTEEN

based on a story by Maureen Daly

Before You Read

Connections

Read the title of the story and study the picture on the left. Describe what you see.

- In what way are the two people in the picture related? Why do you think so?
- Why are they happy? What do you think they have been doing?
- In what way might the telephone be important in the story?
- Describe a time when you took part in a sport. Did you enjoy it? Why or why not?

As you read, think about how the picture connects to the story.

Words to Learn

In this story, you will learn some new words. You will also learn an *idiom*. For example, *all of a sudden* is an idiom that means "without warning."

SIXTEEN

based on a story by Maureen Daly

It was all so lovely.

Now don't get me wrong. I mean, I want you to understand from the beginning that I'm not so dumb. I get around. I read. I watch TV. And I have two older sisters. So, you see, I know what's going on. It's important that you understand that.

You see, it was funny how I met him. It was a winter night like any other winter night. I didn't have my homework done, but the way the moon glistened off the snow drifts, I just couldn't stay inside. The skating rink isn't far from our house—you can make it in five minutes if the sidewalks aren't slippery, so I went skating. I remember it took me a long time to get ready that night because I had trouble finding my skating socks. I don't know why they always disappear.

My skates were hanging by the back door all nice and shiny because I had just gotten them. My dog walked with me as far as the corner. She's a mutt, very polite and well mannered. She panted along beside me and her breath was a frosty little balloon balancing on the end of her nose. My skates thumped me good-naturedly on the back as I walked and the night was breathlessly quiet, and the stars winked down like a million flirting eyes. It was all so lovely.

I began to run. I ran most of the way on the snow covered streets. It was lucky the sidewalks had sand on them or I surely would have slipped. The sand crunched beneath my feet and I could feel the cold through the thinness of my shoes. I always wear old shoes when I go skating. I cut through someone's backyard because that was the shortest way to go. And then I was there.

I was out of breath when I got to the skating rink, out of breath with running and with the chill of the night. Our skating rink is a very friendly place. Inside, the lounge was filled with people talking

and drinking hot chocolate around the fireplace. There was the smell of burning wood in the air as logs slowly turned to ashes. Girls burst through the door laughing, snow on their hair, and tripped over shoes scattered on the floor. A boy grabbed the hat off the girl he was with and stuffed it into an empty pocket to prove his love. Then he hastily bent down to examine his skate strap with innocent unconcern.

It didn't take me long to get my skates on and to put my shoes in the locker. Then I walked outside as the blades of my new skates hugged the ice.

It was snowing lightly, tiny flakes that melted as soon as they touched your hand. I don't know where the snow came from because there were stars in the sky. I kept seeing them every time I looked up into the darkness.

I waited a moment. Starting to skate in a crowded rink is like jumping on a moving merry-go-round. The skaters go gliding round and round to the beat of the rhythm of the music, which echoes in the night. Once I hopped in, it went all right. At least, after I found out how to avoid that rough spot on the ice.

And then there he was. All of a sudden his arm was around my waist and he said very casually, "Mind if I skate with you?" as he took my other hand. That's all there was to it. Just that and then we were skating. It wasn't that I'd never skated with a guy before. Don't be silly. I told you, I get around. But this was different. He was the most popular guy in school. And while I knew who he was, I never would have approached him. I would have been much too intimidated.

At first I can't remember what we talked about. I can't even remember if we talked at all. We just skated and skated and laughed every time we came to that rough spot in the ice, and pretty soon we were laughing all the time at nothing at all.

Then we sat on the big snowbank at the edge of the rink and just watched. He threw a handful of snow at me and it fell in a little white shower on my hair and he leaned over to brush it off. I held my breath. The night stood still.

The moon hung over the ice like a big slice of melon and the smoke from the chimney floated up in a sooty fog. One by one the lights in the houses near the rink went out. Somebody's dog wailed a mournful goodnight to a star and then curled up for the night to go to sleep.

Then he sat up straight and said, "We'd better start home." He didn't say, "Shall I take you home?" or "Do you live far?" but "We'd better start home." See, that's how I knew he wanted to take me home. Not because he *had* to but because he wanted to. He went back inside to get my shoes from the locker.

He was smiling when he came back and took off my skates and tied the wet skate strings in a soggy knot and put them over his shoulder. Then he held out his hand and I slid off the snowbank and brushed the snow off my pants and we were ready.

It was snowing harder now. Big, fluffy flakes that clung to the bushes and quickly covered everything like a blanket. I looked around. The night was a painting in black and white.

It was all so lovely I was sorry that I lived only a few blocks away. He talked softly as we walked, as if every word were a secret. We talked about the kind of music we liked, and if I planned to go to college. It was a very respectable kind of conversation, and then he said how nice I looked with the snow in my hair, and asked if I had ever seen the moon so close. The moon *did* seem to be following us as we walked hand in hand. And then we were home.

The porch light was on. My mother always puts the porch light on when I go out at night. We stood there a few moments by the front steps. Feathery flakes gently settled on his hair. Then he took my skates and put them over my shoulder. "Good night now. I'll call you," he said.

I went inside and watched him from my window as he went down the street. He was whistling softly. I waited until the sound faded away. And then I couldn't see him anymore.

I shivered. Somehow the darkness seemed changed. The stars were little hard chips of light far up in the sky, and the moon stared down with a harsh yellow glare. The air was tense with sudden cold and a gust of wind suddenly erased his footprints into white oblivion. Everything was quiet.

But he said, "I'll call you." That's what he said. "I'll call you." And that thought warmed my heart.

And that was last Thursday. Tonight is Tuesday. Tonight is Tuesday and my homework is done, and I did a crossword puzzle, and I watched TV, and now I'm just sitting. I'm just sitting because I can't think of anything else to do. I can't think of anything, anything but snowflakes and ice skates and yellow moons and Thursday night. The telephone is sitting on the corner table with its face turned to the wall so I can't see it staring at me. I don't even jump when it rings anymore. Outside the night is still, so still I think I'll go crazy. And the white snow is all dirty.

And so I'm just sitting here, and I'm not feeling anything. I'm not even sad because all of a sudden I know. I can sit here and laugh while the tears run salty in the corners of my mouth. For all of a sudden I know what the stars knew all along—he'll never, never call.

A man is saddened by the loss of a loved one.

Bread and Music
Part I from "Discordants"
by Conrad Aiken

Music I heard with you was more than music,
And bread I broke with you was more than bread.
Now that I am without you, all is desolate,[1]
All that was once so beautiful is dead.

Your hands once touched this table and this silver,[2]   5
And I have seen your fingers hold this glass.
These things do not remember you, beloved,
And yet your touch upon them will not pass.

For it was in my heart you moved among them,
And blessed them with your hands and with your eyes.   10
And in my heart they will remember always,—
They knew you once, O beautiful and wise.

1. *desolate:* empty and very unhappy.
2. *silver:* silverware—knives, spoons, and forks.

We all need other people. It's hard to survive by yourself.

Alone
by Maya Angelou

Lying, thinking
Last night
How to find my soul a home
Where water is not thirsty
And bread loaf is not stone   5
I came up with one thing
And I don't believe I'm wrong
That nobody,
But nobody
Can make it out here alone.   10

Alone, all alone
Nobody, but nobody
Can make it out here alone.

There are some millionaires
With money they can't use   15
Their wives run round like banshees[1]
Their children sing the blues
They've got expensive doctors
To cure their hearts of stone.
But nobody   20
No nobody
Can make it out here alone

Alone, all alone
Nobody, but nobody
Can make it out here alone.   25

1. *banshees:* ghosts in the forms of women that warn of death.

Now if you listen closely
I'll tell you what I know
Storm clouds are gathering
The wind is gonna blow
The race of man is suffering   30
And I can hear the moan,
Cause nobody,
But nobody
Can make it out here alone.

Alone, all alone   35
Nobody, but nobody
Can make it out here alone.

Put an *x* in the box next to the correct answer.

Reading Comprehension

1. The story tells about what happened on
  ❏ **a.** a Saturday morning.
  ❏ **b.** a Sunday afternoon.
  ❏ **c.** a winter night.

2. The girl said that the skating rink was
  ❏ **a.** far from her house.
  ❏ **b.** a very friendly place.
  ❏ **c.** usually empty.

3. Who walked to the corner with the girl?
  ❏ **a.** her mother
  ❏ **b.** her brother
  ❏ **c.** her dog

4. Which statement is true?
  ❏ **a.** The two people went to different schools.
  ❏ **b.** The two people spoke about the kind of music they liked.
  ❏ **c.** By the time they got to the girl's house, the porch light was out.

5. At the end of the story, the girl was sure that the boy
  ❏ **a.** would call her in a day.
  ❏ **b.** would call her in a week.
  ❏ **c.** would never call.

Vocabulary

6. The moon glistened off the snow. The word *glistened* means
  ❏ **a.** shone brightly.
  ❏ **b.** was far from.
  ❏ **c.** was dark.

7. She would never talk to him; she was much too intimidated. The word *intimidated* means
  ❏ **a.** brave.
  ❏ **b.** afraid.
  ❏ **c.** sad.

8. Big, fluffy flakes of snow quickly covered everything like a blanket. The word *fluffy* means
  ❏ **a.** hard and tiny.
  ❏ **b.** soft and light.
  ❏ **c.** very dark.

9. A sudden rush of wind erased his footprints from the snow. The word *erased* means
  ❏ **a.** wiped away or removed.
  ❏ **b.** assisted or helped.
  ❏ **c.** froze or turned to ice.

Idioms

10. All of a sudden he was there at her side. The idiom *all of a sudden* means
  ❏ **a.** without warning.
  ❏ **b.** with a loud shout.
  ❏ **c.** with some friends.

How many questions did you answer correctly? Circle your score. Then fill in your score on the Score Chart on page 184.

Number Correct	1	2	3	4	5	6	7	8	9	10
Score	10	20	30	40	50	60	70	80	90	100

EXERCISES TO HELP YOU

Exercise A

Understanding the story. Answer each question with a complete sentence. You may look back at the story.

1. How many older sisters did the girl have?

   _____

   _____

2. How long did it usually take to get to the skating rink?

   _____

   _____

3. Why did it take the girl so long to get ready that night?

   _____

   _____

4. Who or what walked with the girl to the corner?

   _____

   _____

5. What kind of shoes did the girl always wear when she went skating?

   _____

   _____

6. Why didn't the girl slip when she ran on the snowy streets?

   _____

   _____

7. What were the people in the lounge doing?

_____

_____

8. How did she know that the boy wanted to take her home?

_____

_____

9. What did they talk about as they walked to her house?

_____

_____

10. At the end of the story, what did the girl know?

_____

_____

Exercise B

Adding vocabulary. On the left are 8 words from the story. Complete each sentence by adding the correct word.

winked

respectable

soggy

crunched

panted

chips

gust

curled

1. The sand on the sidewalks _____ beneath her feet.

2. The stars _____ down like a million eyes.

3. On the way home, they had a very polite and _____ conversation.

4. Her dog was breathing hard and quickly; it _____ as it walked beside her.

5. A _____ of wind blew by her face, and she suddenly felt cold.

6. The skate strings were very wet. He tied them in a _____ knot.

7. Somebody's dog _____ up for the night to go to sleep.

8. The stars were like little hard _____ of light in the sky.

Exercise C

Adding punctuation. Below is part of a letter the boy might have written to the girl. However, the letter needs 11 **commas**. Add the commas. Then write the corrected letter on the lines.

Dear Maureen

   I wanted to call you last week but I seem to have lost my voice. I really mean that. I woke up Friday with chills a sore throat aches and a fever. Maybe I should have worn a hat gloves and a warmer jacket! I can hardly talk now. However the doctor says I should be better in a couple of days. I'll call you then. I just wanted to say how much I enjoyed skating talking and walking with you.

                                        Your friend

                                        Leon

_____

_____

_____

_____

_____

_____

_____

_____

_____

_____

_____

_____

_____

Exercise D

Finding synonyms. Read each sentence. Then select the **synonym** (the word most similar in meaning) for the word in capital letters. Circle the letter of the correct answer. Each capitalized word appears in the story.

1. She wore warm clothing to protect her from the chill of the night.

   CHILL   **a.** darkness   **b.** danger   **c.** cold

2. Someone tripped over some shoes that were scattered on the floor.

   SCATTERED   **a.** thrown   **b.** cleaned   **c.** taken

3. Since he was the most popular boy at school, she knew who he was.

   POPULAR   **a.** tall   **b.** old   **c.** liked

4. She heard someone's dog as it wailed good night to a star.

   WAILED   **a.** smiled   **b.** cried   **c.** coughed

5. The skates thumped her on the back as she walked along.

   THUMPED   **a.** knocked   **b.** cut   **c.** dropped

6. The moon stared down with a harsh yellow glare.

   GLARE   **a.** heat   **b.** shadow   **c.** brightness

7. When he walked away, she suddenly shivered from the cold.

   SHIVERED   **a.** shook   **b.** shouted   **c.** slipped

Exercise E

Changing statements to questions. Write two questions for each statement. Begin the questions with *Who, What, When, Where, Why,* or *How*. End each question with a question mark. The first one has been done for you.

1. The skates were hanging by the back door.

   a. *What were hanging by the back door?*

   b. *Where were the skates hanging?*

2. The dog walked slowly to the corner.

   a. _____

   b. _____

3. She walked through someone's backyard because that was the fastest way to go.

   a. _____

   b. _____

4. Since there was a fire in the fireplace, the lounge was warm.

   a. _____

   b. _____

5. She was surprised because he was suddenly at her side.

   a. _____

   b. _____

6. They sat on the big snow bank at the edge of the rink.

   a. _____

   b. _____

7. My mother always puts the porch light on at night.

    a. _____

    b. _____

8. Thin, light flakes of snow settled gently on his hair.

    a. _____

    b. _____

9. Last Thursday, Leon said, "I'll call you."

    a. _____

    b. _____

10. I'm sitting here silently because I can't think of anything else to do.

    a. _____

    b. _____

Exercise F

Vocabulary review. Write a complete sentence for each word or group of words.

1. glistened _____

_____

2. erased _____

_____

3. fluffy _____

_____

4. intimidated _____

_____

5. soggy _____

_____

6. respectable _____

_____

7. gust _____

_____

8. popular _____

_____

9. scattered _____

_____

10. all of a sudden _____

_____

SHARING WITH OTHERS

This section provides you with opportunities to share your thoughts and ideas with others, while you practice and improve your reading, writing, speaking, and listening skills.

Part A

Discuss the following questions. Share your answers with your partner or with the group.

1. The setting of a story is where and when the main action takes place. What is the setting of "Sixteen"? Why is the setting so important in this story?

2. Why do you think the girl cared so much about a boy she hardly knew? Offer several reasons.

3. "I'm not even sad," said the girl at the end of the story. What did she mean by these words? How *did* she feel?

4. Is "Sixteen" a sad story or a humorous story—or both? Explain.

5. Tell why you think the story is called "Sixteen."

6. At the conclusion of the story, the girl is convinced that the boy will not call. Are you as certain of that as the girl is? What do you think will happen?

Part B

1. There are many **descriptive passages** in "Sixteen." For example, the author describes the lounge, the skating rink, and the snowy night. **Describe** one of the above. If you prefer, write a description of something else in the story.

_____

_____

_____

_____

_____

_____

_____

_____

_____

_____

_____

_____

_____

_____

2. On the lines below, **summarize** the story.

_____

_____

_____

_____

_____

_____

_____

_____

_____

_____

_____

_____

_____

_____

_____

_____

Part C
Poetry

BREAD AND MUSIC

1. **Stanzas** are lines in a poem that go together. "Bread and Music" contains three stanzas. How many lines are there in each stanza? Which lines in each stanza rhyme?

2. The poem is about the loss of a loved one or someone who is dear. Read stanza 1 again. The poet suggests that when you are in love with someone, everything in life seems better and more wonderful. However, when you have lost someone you love, everything seems sad and dreary. Do you think this is true? Why?

3. Read stanzas 2 and 3 again. Name three things that remind the poet of his loved one. Is this poem humorous or sad? Explain.

ALONE

1. How many stanzas are there in "Alone"? What two lines express the main idea of the poem? Notice how many times these lines are repeated.

2. A **simile** compares two things by using *like* or *as*. Here are some similes that appear in "Sixteen":

    • The stars winked down *like* a million flirting eyes.
    • The moon was *like* a big slice of melon.
    • The snow covered everything *like* a blanket.

    Find a simile in stanza 3 of "Alone."

3. A **metaphor** compares two things without using the words *like* or *as*. Here are two metaphors that appear in "Sixteen":

    • The dog's breath was a frosty little balloon.
    • The stars were hard chips of light.

    Find a metaphor in stanza 3 of "Alone." (Hint: What are millionaires' hearts?)

4. "Alone" suggests that everyone needs other people. Why do you think this poem appears in a unit with "Sixteen" and "Bread and Music"?

THE STOLEN LETTER

based on a story by Edgar Allan Poe

Before You Read

Connections

Study the picture on the left. Describe what you see.
- Does this story take place in the past or the present? How do you know?
- Why is the bearded man looking through a microscope?
- Why do you think one of the men is wearing dark glasses?
- Do you prefer stories that take place in the present or in the past? Tell why.

As you read, think about how the picture connects to the story.

Words to Learn

In this story, you will learn some new words. You will also learn some idioms. For example, *in vain* is an idiom that means "useless."

THE STOLEN LETTER

based on a story by Edgar Allan Poe

The man was clever—but not clever enough.

In Paris, one freezing winter evening, I was having dinner with my good friend, C. Auguste Dupin, the famous detective. We had just finished our meal, when there was a loud knocking at the door. Dupin opened it. There stood Mr. Germain, the Chief of the Paris Police.

We welcomed him warmly, for he was an old acquaintance whom we had not seen for a long time.

"I need your assistance," said Germain. "I would like your opinion about a case I am working on now. It has been giving me a great deal of trouble."

"Please sit down," said Dupin, as he pointed to a comfortable chair.

"The case is simple," said Germain. "It is *very* simple, indeed. And yet it is very strange."

"You say the case is simple and strange?" said Dupin.

"Yes. The truth is we are puzzled because the case *is* so simple, and yet, at the same time, it has baffled us completely."

"Tell us about it," said Dupin.

"Before I begin," said the Chief, "let me caution you to keep this secret. If anyone found out that I confided this to you, I would certainly lose my job."

"All right. Go on."

"Well, then," said the Chief, "I have received information from a highly placed person in the government. I have learned that a very important letter has been stolen from an office in the royal palace. We know who stole it. There is no question about that, for the man

was seen taking it. We also know that he still has the letter."

"But who would dare do such a thing!" I exclaimed.

"The thief," said Germain softly, "is a man who dares to do many dangerous things. He is one of the most powerful and important ministers in the government. He is Minister Danton!"

Dupin shook his head and then whistled softly.

"Every day," said the Chief, "it becomes more and more important to obtain the letter. You see, its contents could be extremely embarrassing to the government. Therefore, it is important to get the letter back as soon as possible. The case has been given to me. I am personally responsible for finding the letter and returning it."

"Are you sure," I asked, "that the Minister still has the letter?"

"I am sure of that," said the Chief. "Therefore, my first move was to search the Minister's house. The problem was that I had to search the house without his knowing it. I had been warned of the danger that would result from giving him reason to suspect our plan."

"But," said Dupin, "you are an expert in these investigations. You have done this many times before."

"Oh, yes," said the Chief. "And because of that I was confident of success. The Minister's habits were helpful to me too. He is usually away from his home all day, and I have keys, as you know, that can open any door in Paris. Every day for the past three weeks, I have been personally involved in searching his house. After all, my reputation is at stake! Not only that, but there is an enormous reward. So I looked everywhere in the house. I checked every place where it might be hidden. I searched every corner and crack where the letter could possibly be concealed. I finally abandoned the search when I was convinced that it was not possible to find the letter. This man, Danton, is even more clever than I thought."

"But isn't it possible," I suggested, "that the Minister has hidden the letter somewhere outside the house?"

"That is not possible," said the Chief. "It would be far too dangerous. Besides, I have agents who watch him all the time."

"Then the letter must still be in the house," I said. "But could the Minister have the letter with him?"

"Not at all," said the Chief. "I have arranged twice to have him robbed. Both times he was carefully searched and nothing was found."

"You might have saved yourself the trouble," said Dupin. "Danton is no fool. He must have anticipated that he would be searched and would have been prepared for that."

"Why don't you tell us how you searched his house," I said.

"We took our time," said the Chief, "and we searched *everywhere*. As I said, I have a great deal of experience in this sort of thing. We carefully searched the entire house, room by room, spending many days in each. First we looked at the furniture in each room. We opened every drawer. And, as you know, to a well-trained police officer, such a thing as a 'secret' drawer is impossible. Next we inspected the chairs. We used long, thin needles to see if anything had been hidden in the cushions. Then we removed the tops from the tables."

"Why did you do that?" I asked.

"Sometimes the top of a table, or other piece of furniture, is removed by a person who wishes to hide something inside. Then the leg is hollowed out, the article is put into the cavity, and the top is put back on."

"But," said I, "you could not possibly have taken apart *every* piece of furniture in which it would have been possible to hide the letter. After all, a letter may be rolled up very tightly until it is as thin as a pencil. Then it could be hidden, for example, in the hollowed out back of a chair. You did not take apart all the chairs in the house, did you?"

"No, but we did even better. With a powerful microscope, we examined the wood on every piece of furniture in the house. If there had been the slightest sign that it had been recently disturbed, we would have detected it immediately. Under the microscope, a few grains of dust would have looked as large as apples. A drop of glue would have been obvious to us."

"I presume you checked the mirrors and beds, the clothing in the closets, the rugs, and the curtains."

"All that, of course. In fact, we examined *every* item in the house. We divided the house into squares and gave each square a number. Then we carefully inspected each square with the powerful microscope I mentioned to you before."

"You looked among Danton's papers, of course, and at his books?"

"Certainly. We not only opened every book, but we turned over every page. We examined the covers of the books and the backs of the books too."

"You looked at the floor underneath the carpets?"

"Absolutely. We removed every carpet and checked the floor boards underneath them."

"And the wallpaper?"

"Yes."

"You looked in the basement?"

"We did. In fact, we even checked the grounds around the house. Everything was covered with bricks. That made it very easy for us. We examined the moss between the bricks and found it had not been touched."

"Well, you certainly went to a great deal of trouble," I said.

"Yes," replied the Chief, "but as I told you before, the reward is enormous."

"Then," I said, "I guess you were mistaken about the letter, and that it is not hidden in the house."

"I am afraid you are right," said the Chief. Then turning to Dupin, he asked, "What would you advise me to do?"

Without pausing for a moment, Dupin responded, "Search the house again."

"But," said the Chief, "as sure as I am breathing, the letter is not there!"

"That is the best advice I can give you," said Dupin. "Oh, by the way, you have, I guess, a good description of the letter?"

"Oh, yes," said the Chief. He pulled a small black notebook out of his pocket. Then, slowly and carefully, he proceeded to read aloud an accurate description of the missing letter. When he finished reading, he left. I had never seen the man so unhappy and depressed.

About a month later, I received a message from Auguste Dupin. The great detective had written, "This is to inform you that I have asked Chief Germain to meet me at seven o'clock this evening. Why don't you come by then? I think that you'll find it very interesting."

When I arrived, Dupin greeted me at the door. "Ah, you're exactly on time," he said. "And there is Chief Germain, just a few steps behind you."

The three of us chatted pleasantly for a while. Finally, I asked the Chief, "Whatever happened to that stolen letter?"

"Well," he said, a little sadly, "I went back, as Dupin suggested, and searched the house again. But, as I knew in advance, it was all in vain. We did not find the letter."

"How much was the reward, did you say?" asked Dupin.

"Why, a very great deal—it's a *very* large reward. I don't want to say precisely how much. But there's one thing I *will* say. I would gladly give my personal check for fifty thousand francs to anyone who could get me that letter. I mean it. I would happily give fifty thousand francs to get my hands on that letter."

"In that case," said Dupin, "you can write me a check for the amount you mentioned. And after you have signed it, I will hand you the letter."

I was astonished. The Chief stood there with his mouth open, staring at Dupin. The Chief finally recovered. He grabbed a pen,

wrote a check for fifty thousand francs, and handed it to Dupin.
Dupin looked at the check carefully and put it in his wallet. Then,
unlocking his desk, he took out a letter and handed it to the Chief.
With a trembling hand, Germain unfolded the letter, glanced at the
words, and dashed wildly out of the room. He had not uttered a
syllable since Dupin asked him to write the check.

When I got over my shock, I turned to Dupin and said, "Please
be good enough to explain."

"With great pleasure," said the master detective. "With very
great pleasure. I know that the Paris police are very capable. They
are hardworking and smart, and they do their job very well. But in
this case, they searched for the letter the wrong way."

"What do you mean?" I asked.

"Don't you see?" said Dupin. "In searching for the letter, the
Chief and his officers thought only about how *they* would have
hidden it. The Chief believes that *everyone* would hide a letter in
some secret out-of-the-way place—in the leg of a table or under the
carpet. And if it *had* been hidden in a place like that, I am sure that
the police would have found it.

"But I know Minister Danton very well. He is a *very* intelligent man. He knew that his house would be searched. He knew that the searchers would use a powerful microscope. And, therefore, he knew that he could not hide the letter in any of the usual hiding places. I realized, then, that the Minister might have left the letter out in the open, *right under everyone's nose*, where no one would search for it. The more I thought about the case, the more convinced I became that the Minister had hidden the letter by not hiding it at all!

"With this idea in mind, I put on a pair of dark glasses, and went, early one morning, to the Minister's house. I found the Minister at home and he led me to his study. Once there, I complained about my weak eyes, which forced me, I said, to wear the dark glasses. The dark glasses, you understand, enabled me to look carefully around the room without permitting the Minister to realize I was doing that.

"All the time, while I pretended to be interested in what the Minister was saying, I was really looking around the room. I saw nothing suspicious until my eyes stopped, suddenly, on a cardboard letter holder on a wooden shelf over the fireplace. The letter holder had three compartments. In them were several cards and a letter. The letter was soiled and crumpled and was torn nearly in half. It looked as though someone had started tearing it up and had changed his mind. The letter was addressed to the Minister in small, neat handwriting. The letter seemed to have been dropped, without much thought, into the letter rack.

"As soon as I saw that letter, I was certain that it was the one I was seeking! It is true that this letter looked very different from the one that the Minister had described to us. That letter was addressed, in large handwriting, to an important official in the government. This letter was addressed, in small handwriting, to Minister Danton. But the letter here was soiled, crumpled, and torn—unusual for the Minister, who is so careful and neat. And the fact that the letter was there—out in the open where anyone could easily see it—that made me very suspicious!"

"So what did you do?"

"I kept talking to the Minister about a subject that I knew he found fascinating. But all the time I kept staring at the letter, memorizing exactly how it looked and exactly where it was placed in the holder. And then I saw something that convinced me I was right!"

"What was that?" I asked.

"I noticed that the folds in the letter seemed to be a bit worn. It was as though the letter had been folded, and then folded again, *in the opposite direction.* I realized then that the letter had been turned inside out, like a glove, and had been addressed again, on the other side!"

"What did you do then?"

"I said good-bye to the Minister and departed. But I purposely left one of my gloves behind."

"So that you would have a reason to come back!"

Dupin nodded. "The next morning I returned for my glove. While the Minister and I were talking, we suddenly heard loud shots coming from outside. The Minister rushed to the window, opened it and looked out. As he did, I hurried to the letter holder. I quickly took the letter and put it into my pocket. Then I replaced it with another letter that looked exactly like the first.

"The shots in the street, it seems, had been caused by some fool who was firing a gun. But since he was shooting blanks, no one was hurt. The 'fool,' of course, was a man I had hired to create a disturbance. A few minutes later, I said good-bye to the Minister and left."

"Well done!" I cried. "But tell me this. Why did you bother to go back to replace the letter with one that looked just like it? When you saw the letter on your first visit, why didn't you simply grab it and run?"

"Minister Danton," replied Dupin, "is a very dangerous man. When he is at home, there is always an armed guard somewhere in the house. If I had made the wild attempt you just suggested, I might never have left his place alive. The people of Paris might never have seen me again."

Dupin paused thoughtfully, smiled, and then said, "I wish, however, I could see the look on the Minister's face when he finally opens the letter I left."

"Why? Did you write something special?"

"It did not seem right to leave the inside of the letter blank. So I wrote in these words:

> *Your plan was good, but mine was better.*
> *As you can see, I took the letter.*"

You Can Answer These Questions

Put an *x* in the box next to the correct answer.

Reading Comprehension

1. Chief Germain visited Dupin because the Chief wanted to
   - ❏ **a.** ask for his help.
   - ❏ **b.** have dinner with him.
   - ❏ **c.** borrow some money.

2. Germain got into the Minister's house by
   - ❏ **a.** climbing through a window.
   - ❏ **b.** breaking down the door.
   - ❏ **c.** using one of his many keys.

3. The Chief gave Dupin a check for
   - ❏ **a.** 25,000 francs.
   - ❏ **b.** 50,000 francs.
   - ❏ **c.** 100,000 francs.

4. When he went to the Minister's house, Dupin wore dark glasses because he
   - ❏ **a.** liked the way he looked in them.
   - ❏ **b.** had weak eyes.
   - ❏ **c.** didn't want the Minister to know that he was looking around.

5. The Minister "hid" the letter
   - ❏ **a.** in a letter holder.
   - ❏ **b.** in the leg of a table.
   - ❏ **c.** in a secret drawer.

6. The shots were fired by
   - ❏ **a.** a man who was crazy.
   - ❏ **b.** a man Dupin had hired.
   - ❏ **c.** Chief Germain.

Vocabulary

7. He was an old acquaintance they had not seen for a while. An *acquaintance* is
   - ❏ **a.** a soldier.
   - ❏ **b.** an enemy.
   - ❏ **c.** a person whom one knows.

8. The Chief abandoned the search when he was certain that he would not find the letter. The word *abandoned* means
   - ❏ **a.** started over.
   - ❏ **b.** looked for.
   - ❏ **c.** gave up completely.

9. Germain was unhappy and depressed. As used here, the word *depressed* means
   - ❏ **a.** friendly.
   - ❏ **b.** cheerful.
   - ❏ **c.** sad.

Idioms

10. He searched the house again, but he knew it would be in vain. The idiom *in vain* means
    - ❏ **a.** useless.
    - ❏ **b.** helpful.
    - ❏ **c.** interesting.

How many questions did you answer correctly? Circle your score. Then fill in your score on the Score Chart on page 184.

Number Correct	1	2	3	4	5	6	7	8	9	10
Score	10	20	30	40	50	60	70	80	90	100

Exercise A

Understanding the story. Answer each question with a complete sentence. You may look back at the story.

1. According to the Chief, who stole the letter?

   _____

   _____

2. From where was the letter stolen?

   _____

   _____

3. When the Chief learned that the letter had been stolen, what was the first thing that he did?

   _____

   _____

4. How did the Chief know that the Minister did not have the letter with him?

   _____

   _____

5. What did the police use to examine the wood on the furniture in the house?

   _____

   _____

6. How much was the check that the Chief gave Dupin?

   _____

   _____

7. Why did Dupin wear dark glasses when he went to the Minister's house?

_____

_____

8. Where had the Minister put the letter?

_____

_____

9. Why did the Minister rush to the window?

_____

_____

10. What did Dupin do when the Minister was looking out the window?

_____

_____

_____

Exercise B

Adding vocabulary. On the left are 8 words from the story. Complete each sentence by adding the correct word.

reward

baffled

disturbance

cavity

confident

moss

anticipated

confided

1. The Chief was sure that he would succeed. He was

   _____ of success.

2. Although the case appeared to be simple, it

   _____ nearly everyone.

3. The Chief said, "I will lose my job if anyone finds out

   that I _____ this to you."

4. The person who returns the letter will receive a

   large _____.

5. Since the Minister _____ that he

   would be searched, he was prepared for that.

6. Sometimes a person makes a hole in a piece of

   wood and then hides something in the

   _____ .

7. The police carefully looked at the

   _____ between the bricks in the

   street.

8. Dupin paid a man to create a _____

   by firing a gun.

Exercise C

Adding punctuation. An **appositive** is a noun that adds information about another noun that appears before it.

noun   appositive
Mrs. Rodriguez, my teacher, is in room 209.

noun   appositive
Let me introduce Mrs. Rodriguez, my teacher.

Usually, an appositive is separated from the rest of the sentence by a comma or commas.

Each of the following sentences contains an appositive. Add a comma, or commas, where needed. Write the corrected sentence on the line. The first one has been done for you.

1. Auguste Dupin the famous detective invited me to join him for dinner.

   Auguste Dupin, the famous detective, invited me to join him for dinner.

2. Mr. Germain the Chief of the Paris Police knocked on the door.

   _____

   _____

3. Minister Danton a very important man stole the letter.

   _____

   _____

4. The story takes place in Paris one of the most beautiful cities in the world.

   _____

   _____

5. Minister Danton a very intelligent person knew that his house would be searched.

   _____

   _____

6. Dupin a brilliant detective found the stolen letter.

_____

_____

7. Edgar Allan Poe the great American writer is the author of several

detective stories.

_____

_____

8. Poe was born in Boston a city in Massachusetts.

_____

_____

9. Pat my best friend has read this story many times.

_____

_____

10. Pat's father a teacher sometimes discusses the story in class.

_____

_____

Exercise D

Finding synonyms. Read each sentence. Then select the **synonym** (the word most similar in meaning) for the word in capital letters. Circle the letter of the correct answer. Each capitalized word appears in the story.

1. Chief Germain asked Auguste Dupin for assistance with a case.

   ASSISTANCE   **a.** help   **b.** cash   **c.** books

2. The Chief had experience in these kinds of investigations.

   INVESTIGATIONS **a.** offices   **b.** searches   **c.** notes

3. If the letter had been hidden in a chair, they would have detected that immediately.

   DETECTED   **a.** discovered   **b.** forgotten   **c.** destroyed

4. The police searched the grounds around the house.

   GROUNDS   **a.** windows   **b.** homes   **c.** land

5. The letter was concealed somewhere in the house.

   CONCEALED   **a.** hidden   **b.** torn   **c.** lost

6. He wrote, "This is to inform you that I have asked Chief Germain to meet me at seven o'clock this evening."

   INFORM   **a.** ask   **b.** surprise   **c.** tell

7. Although the reward was large, Germain did not say precisely how much it was.

   PRECISELY   **a.** loudly   **b.** joyfully   **c.** exactly

8. The three men sat down and chatted pleasantly.

   CHATTED   **a.** ate   **b.** talked   **c.** argued

9. When Dupin said he had the letter, the Chief was astonished. His mouth hung open, and he couldn't say a word.

   ASTONISHED   **a.** angry   **b.** sorry   **c.** amazed

10. Dupin kept staring at the letter. He was memorizing exactly how it looked and exactly where it was.

   MEMORIZING   **a.** saying   **b.** remembering   **c.** wondering

Exercise E

Part A

Building sentences. Combine two **simple sentences** into one **complex sentence** by using the **subordinating conjunction** in parentheses. Begin the sentence with the conjunction, and use a comma at the end of the **clause**. Write the complex sentence on the line. The first one has been done for you.

Common Subordinating Conjunctions

after	since	although
when	if	while

1. The case was simple. It was very strange. (although)

   Although the case was simple, it was very strange.

2. We finished eating dinner. There was a loud knocking at the door. (after)

   _____

   _____

3. The Minister expected to be searched. He was prepared for that. (since)

   _____

   _____

4. The Chief looked everywhere for the letter. He could not find it. (although)

   _____

   _____

5. The Minister is very intelligent. He knew that he could not hide the letter in the usual hiding places. (since)

   _____

   _____

   _____

6. You can give me a check for fifty thousand francs. I will give you the letter. (if)

_____

_____

7. He pretended to be interested in the Minister's words. He was really looking around the room. (while)

_____

_____

_____

8. I got over my shock. I asked Dupin to explain. (when)

_____

_____

9. The Minister and I were talking. We suddenly heard loud shots. (while)

_____

_____

10. The Minister ran to the window. Dupin took the letter. (when)

_____

_____

Part B

Combine two **simple sentences** into one **complex sentence** by using
the **subordinating conjunctions** below. Begin the sentence with the
conjunction, and use a comma at the end of the **clause**. Write the
complex sentence on the line. Use each conjunction once.

after   **although**   **since**   **while**

11. Germain looked at the letter. He ran wildly out of the room.

_____

_____

12. Dupin left a glove at the Minister's house. He had to return to get it.

_____

_____

13. The Minister was away from his house. The police searched it.

_____

_____

14. The Minister's plan was good. Dupin's plan was better.

_____

_____

Exercise F

Vocabulary review. Write a complete sentence for each word or group of words.

1. acquaintance _____

   _____

2. abandoned _____

   _____

3. confident _____

   _____

4. reward _____

   _____

5. concealed _____

   _____

6. detected _____

   _____

7. astonished _____

   _____

8. disturbance _____

   _____

9. anticipated _____

   _____

10. in vain _____

   _____

SHARING WITH OTHERS

This section provides you with opportunities to share your thoughts and ideas with others, while you practice and improve your reading, writing, speaking, and listening skills.

Part A

Discuss the following questions. Share your answers with your partner or with the group.

1. Chief Germain said that the case was both simple and confusing. Why did he think that the case would be simple? Why was it confusing?

2. Why did Germain personally search the house? Why do you think he decided to visit C. Auguste Dupin?

3. The more Dupin thought about the case, the more convinced he became that "the Minister had hidden the letter by not hiding it at all." How could the Minister hide the letter by not hiding it at all?

4. Dupin was able to solve the case by putting himself in the Minister's shoes. What do you do when you "put yourself in someone else's shoes"? Explain how doing that helped Dupin. Have you ever "put yourself in some else's shoes"? If so, tell what happened.

5. After he visited the Minister, Dupin must have
    a. prepared a letter like the one he had seen in the cardboard letter holder.
    b. told a man where and when to fire a gun.
    c. written a brief poem.

    Which of these do you think was the most important? Which was the least important? Why?

6. When the Minister reads the poem, do you think he will know that it was written by Dupin? Explain.

Part B

1. Make a list of all the things the police did when they searched the
Minister's house. You will probably want to look back at the story.

The things the police did when they searched the minister's house

1. _____

_____

_____

_____

_____

_____

_____

_____

_____

_____

_____

_____

_____

_____

_____

_____

_____

2. Now write Chief Germain's report of the investigation. The report should **summarize** the list you just made.

Chief Germain's Report

_____

_____

_____

_____

_____

_____

_____

_____

_____

_____

_____

_____

_____

_____

_____

_____

_____

_____

THE SANCTUARY

based on a story by Jesse Stuart

Connections

Study the picture on the left. Describe what you see.

- How does the woman feel? How do you know?
- Who do you think is sitting in the chair? Why do you think so?
- A sanctuary is a place that provides safety and protection. What do you think the sanctuary is in the story?
- Does the woman in the picture remind you of someone you know? Describe that person.

As you read, think about how the picture connects to the story.

Words to Learn

In this story, you will learn some new words. You will also learn an idiom. For example, *all at once* is an idiom that means "suddenly."

THE SANCTUARY

based on a story by Jesse Stuart

Grandma was determined to stay in her old house.

After Grandpa died, Grandma lived alone in her big house that stood on a high hill surrounded by giant trees. Grandma was old, and she was so crippled with rheumatism she could hardly move around. But she decided to stay in her big house even though it looked as though it was ready to collapse.

"Your mother can't go on living in that house," Pa told Mom. "That house is old. It's ready to crash down. She must come and live with us."

"But Ma will never leave that house," Mom said. "She was born in it. She was married in it. Her seven children were born in it. Grandpa planted that oak tree in front of it when he was a young man. She'll never leave that house."

"I'll go up there now and see her," Pa said to Mom. "I'll explain it to her."

"I'd like to go with you, Pa," I said.

"All right," he said.

We lived close to Grandma. If it weren't for the apple orchard[1] that Pa had planted, we could have seen Grandma's house from our house. We lived just a quarter of a mile away.

When we reached the front gate, Pa stood and looked at it. "This gate is ready to fall," Pa said, as he opened it very carefully. Then he stood and stared at the huge oak tree in the front yard. The tree was so rotten inside, it looked as though the next storm would knock it down. Birds had built their nests in its hollow.

---

1. *orchard:* a piece of land on which fruit trees are grown.

Then Pa looked up at the roof. He said, "That roof is ready to cave in."

But I knew that Grandma wouldn't let Pa or my uncles fix the roof. She wouldn't let them remove an old board and put a new one on. She said it was her roof and she was satisfied with it the way it was.

As we entered the house, Pa smiled and said, "Hello, Mother. I thought I'd come by to see how you're feeling."

"I feel all right, Mick," she said. Grandma looked at me and asked, "How are you, Shan?"

"I'm fine," I said.

"Your gate needs to be fixed, Mother," said Pa. "It's about ready to fall down."

"That gate is all right," Grandma said. "Nephew Herbert fixed that gate for me. He fixed it just the way I wanted it."

"But what about that big oak tree in the front yard?" Pa asked her. "Any windstorm is liable to push that tree over onto the house."

"I've got birds that have built nests in that oak for twenty-five years," Grandma said. "I don't want to have it cut down. Let it fall on the house if it doesn't find some other place to fall."

Pa didn't say anything. Finally Grandma said, "If you all are afraid that I am going to be found dead in this house some morning, I don't mind going to your house, and I'll try staying there for a while. I'll still be able to see my house. I've only lived away from this house for three days in my whole life. But going to your house may work out. I'll try it."

So Grandma came to stay with us. Pa took some of her furniture and put it in the room that Mom had set aside for her.

Grandma would sit all day and look through the window at her house. But she really couldn't see it very well because one of our apple trees was in the way. After a week went by, Grandma became very homesick. When I was sitting in the room with her, she suddenly told me that she wanted me to cut down the apple tree in our orchard so that she could see her house better. I told Mom about it and she told me not to do it.

"I know your Pa doesn't want it cut. I don't want it cut either."

Our apple orchard was only eight years old, and the trees had been very carefully trimmed. I knew that our orchard was the prettiest thing on our farm and that it was very valuable to us because it was our main source of income. I wanted to see Grandma get what she wanted, but I knew how hard Mom and Pa had worked on the orchard. I remembered how they set fires near the orchard to make smoke so the frost wouldn't kill the fruit that was still in the blossoms.

Pa came home at noon. After he had fed his team of horses, he came into the house. Mom told him that Grandma wanted us to cut the apple tree so that she would be able to see her house.

"I can't cut one of my flowering fruit trees," Pa said. "I just can't do that."

Pa didn't think about the tree until two days later when he went to work in the orchard. He stopped, threw up his hands, and ran back to the house.

"What's the matter, Mick?" Mom asked.

"Who cut the apple tree?"

"No one," Mom said. "Has it been cut?"

"See for yourself," he told Mom. When Mom went with him to look at the tree, I went to Grandma's room and saw her looking out of the window at her old house. Grandma sat peacefully by the window as if nothing had happened.

I saw Mom and Pa standing by the tree. Pa was carefully

examining it. I went out to see if the tree had been pulled out by a windstorm. And it had. It had been uprooted by a windstorm that had swept around the corner of our orchard and had hit the tree that Grandma had wanted cut down. Not a branch on any of the other trees had been damaged.

"I don't understand this," Pa said. "I think we better take Mother back to her own home. I don't know what might happen here next if we don't."

Grandma was sitting by the window when Pa and Mom asked her if she wanted to move back.

"I never really wanted to move here in the first place," Grandma said. "Yes, take me back."

I was glad when Pa and Mom moved Grandma and her furniture back to her old house. I was glad because then my sister Mary and I could visit her there.

In the spring and summer we went to see Grandma. Then autumn came and the leaves started to fall. They fell into the drainpipes[2] and clogged them, so I climbed on top of the house and pulled the clumps of leaves out of the drainpipes. Once, when I stepped on the roof, my foot broke through. But I never lost my balance or felt that I was in any peril.

I had the best times I ever had in my life when I visited Grandma. I enjoyed the freedom that she gave me. But it made me sad when she said that she would never leave her house again—that

2. *drainpipes:* gutters that carry water away from the house.

she had left it once and that was enough. It hurt me to hear her say that she would die in this house.

One hot September night thunder shook the earth and streaks of lightning cut through the dark sky. It was a terrible night and fierce gusts of wind came. Grandma told Mary and me to leave the house. She said that she would follow us. We didn't want to go first, but she told us to and we did as we were told.

We hadn't gotten beyond the sidewalk when all at once we heard a mighty crash. Little pieces of oak twigs hit us. We ran out into the yard—out into the thick darkness, screaming for Grandma. But she didn't come. The heavy oak tree had fallen onto the decaying house and had crashed through it! When the lightning flashed we could see that parts of the house were still standing, but the doorway that we had come through had collapsed.

"Let's hurry and tell Mom and Pa!" Mary said.

We followed the path toward home by the lightning flashes, and on the way we met Mom and Pa coming in raincoats and carrying lanterns.

"The old oak tree fell on the house!" Mary screamed. "Grandma can't get out!"

When we got to the house, Pa made his way through the pieces of broken shingles and wood and went to the place where Mary told him Grandma was when the crash came. And they found Grandma pinned to the floor underneath a beam.

She was dead. She had died where she wanted to die and maybe the way she had wanted to die. She had died in her own house. The old rotting oak that Pa had often told her was dangerous, and had wanted to cut for her, had killed Grandma. And out into the mighty storm—out into the wind, darkness, and rain—her birds flew from the hollow of the oak. They were singing a mournful song for her.

The poet wishes she were as strong as her grandmothers.

Lineage[1]
by Margaret Walker

My grandmothers were strong.
They followed plows and bent to toil.
They moved through fields sowing seed.
They touched earth and grain grew.
They were full of sturdiness and singing.   5
My grandmothers were strong.

My grandmothers are full of memories
Smelling of soap and onions and wet clay
With veins rolling roughly over quick hands
They have many clean words to say.   10
My grandmothers were strong.
Why am I not as they?

1. *lineage:* family line; ancestors.

She longed for the gift of courage.

The Courage That My Mother Had
by Edna St. Vincent Millay

The courage that my mother had
Went with her, and is with her still:
Rock from New England quarried;[1]
Now granite[2] in a granite hill.

The golden brooch[3] my mother wore   5
She left behind for me to wear;
I have no thing I treasure more:
Yet, it is something I could spare.

Oh, if instead she'd left me
The thing she took into the grave!—   10
That courage like a rock, which she
Has no more need of, and I have.

1. *quarried:* dug from a pit.
2. *granite:* a hard rock.
3. *brooch:* a piece of jewelry that usually is worn near the neck and attached with a pin.

YOU CAN ANSWER THESE QUESTIONS

Put an *x* in the box next to the correct answer.

Reading Comprehension

1. Pa thought that Grandma's house was
    - ❑ **a.** too small for her.
    - ❑ **b.** too cold for her.
    - ❑ **c.** going to crash down.

2. Pa didn't fix the roof on Grandma's house because
    - ❑ **a.** Grandma wouldn't let him fix it.
    - ❑ **b.** he was too lazy to fix it.
    - ❑ **c.** he didn't have enough money to fix it.

3. Which statement is true?
    - ❑ **a.** Grandma wanted to move out of her house.
    - ❑ **b.** Birds built their nests in the old oak tree.
    - ❑ **c.** Shan didn't like to visit Grandma.

4. Grandma asked Shan to cut down the apple tree because she
    - ❑ **a.** wanted to see her house better.
    - ❑ **b.** didn't like apple trees.
    - ❑ **c.** wanted the apples from the tree.

5. The apple tree was pulled up by
    - ❑ **a.** Pa.
    - ❑ **b.** Shan.
    - ❑ **c.** a storm.

6. What killed Grandma?
    - ❑ **a.** old age
    - ❑ **b.** an oak tree
    - ❑ **c.** rheumatism

Vocabulary

7. The old house looked as though it was ready to collapse. The word *collapse* means
    - ❑ **a.** stand forever.
    - ❑ **b.** begin to shake.
    - ❑ **c.** fall down.

8. The apple orchard was the family's main source of income. The word *income* means
    - ❑ **a.** money.
    - ❑ **b.** happiness.
    - ❑ **c.** food.

9. The tree fell on the decaying old house and crashed through the roof. Something that is *decaying* is
    - ❑ **a.** getting stronger.
    - ❑ **b.** getting weaker.
    - ❑ **c.** very beautiful.

Idioms

10. After they left the house they heard, all at once, a mighty crash. The idiom *all at once* means
    - ❑ **a.** all together.
    - ❑ **b.** later.
    - ❑ **c.** suddenly.

How many questions did you answer correctly? Circle your score. Then fill in your score on the Score Chart on page 184.

Number Correct	1	2	3	4	5	6	7	8	9	10
Score	10	20	30	40	50	60	70	80	90	100

Exercise A

Understanding the story. Answer each question with a complete sentence. You may look back at the story.

1. Why was it hard for Grandma to move around?

   _____

   _____

2. Why did Pa want Grandma to leave her house?

   _____

   _____

3. Who planted the oak tree in front of Grandma's house?

   _____

   _____

4. Why didn't Grandma want to have the oak tree cut down?

   _____

   _____

5. Why didn't Pa or the uncles fix Grandma's roof?

   _____

   _____

6. Why did Grandma ask Shan to cut down the apple tree in the orchard?

   _____

   _____

7. What happened to the tree that Grandma wanted Shan to cut down?

_____

_____

8. Why did Shan like to visit Grandma?

_____

_____

9. Where did they find Grandma after the terrible storm?

_____

_____

10. What killed Grandma?

_____

_____

Exercise B

Adding vocabulary. On the left are 8 words from the story. Complete each sentence by adding the correct word.

surrounded

balance

blossoms

peril

crippled

beam

clumps

trimmed

1. Grandma was so _____ that she could hardly move around.

2. The house stood on a high hill _____ by giant trees.

3. When Shan's foot broke through the roof, he didn't lose his _____.

4. They set fires so the frost wouldn't kill the fruit that was still in the _____.

5. The orchard was the prettiest thing on the farm because all of the trees had been carefully _____.

6. Shan pulled the _____ of leaves out of the drainpipes.

7. Although Shan climbed on top of the house, he didn't think he was in any _____.

8. They found Grandma on the floor underneath a heavy _____.

Exercise C

Using verbs correctly. Fill in each blank using the **past tense** of the irregular verbs in parentheses. The first one has been done for you.

1. When Pa _____*went*_____ to see Grandma, he _____*stood*_____ at her front gate. (go, stand)

2. Grandma _____ her house and _____ to live with us. (leave, come)

3. I _____ that Grandma _____ old. (know, be)

4. Grandma _____ that she _____ fine. (say, feel)

5. Pa _____ to Grandma's house and _____ back some of her furniture. (drive, bring)

6. When Grandma was at our house, she _____ and

   _____ very little. (eat, drink)

7. After Grandma _____ a week in our house, she

   _____ very homesick. (spend, get)

8. A whirlwind _____ the apple tree that _____ at the corner of our orchard. (strike, grow)

9. When Pa _____ the apple tree, he _____ up

   his hands and _____ back to the house. (see, throw, run)

10. Pa _____ us he was afraid of what _____ happen if he didn't take Grandma back to her house. (tell, may)

11. Grandma _____ back to the old house and

    _____ in her own room. (ride, sleep)

12. We _____ sad when we _____ Grandma say

    she _____ she would never leave her house again. (be, hear, think)

13. I _____ fun at Grandma's house, and I enjoyed the

freedom that she _____ me. (have, give)

14. I slipped when I _____ to remove the leaves, but I never

_____ my balance. (begin, lose)

15. When the thunder crashed, Mary _____ Shan's hand and

_____ it tightly. (take, hold)

16. We _____ Ma and Pa on the path, and they

_____ us to the house. (meet, lead)

17. Pa _____ his way through the broken wood and

_____ Grandma on the floor. (make, find)

18. We all _____ that Grandma _____
what she had to do. (understand, do)

19. Birds had _____ their nests in the tree that _____
on the house. (build, fall)

20. The birds _____ a sad song when they _____
out of the tree. (sing, fly)

Exercise D

Finding synonyms. Read each sentence. Then select the **synonym** (the word most similar in meaning) for the word in capital letters. Circle the letter of the correct answer. Each capitalized word appears in the story.

1. The tree was so rotten inside, Pa was afraid that the next storm would knock it down.

   ROTTEN   **a.** spoiled   **b.** solid   **c.** wide

2. Grandma thought that her roof was fine. She was satisfied with it exactly as it was.

   SATISFIED   **a.** worried   **b.** protected   **c.** pleased

3. Pa was carefully examining the apple tree in the orchard.

   EXAMINING   **a.** studying   **b.** climbing   **c.** cutting

4. The tree had been uprooted during a windstorm.

   UPROOTED   **a.** saved   **b.** torn out   **c.** helped

5. Not a branch on any of the other trees had been damaged.

   DAMAGED   **a.** missed   **b.** needed   **c.** harmed

6. The leaves clogged the drainpipes, so Shan climbed onto the roof and pulled the leaves out.

   CLOGGED   **a.** filled   **b.** broke   **c.** touched

7. After Grandma died, the birds sang a mournful song for her.

   MOURNFUL   **a.** joyous   **b.** sad   **c.** loud

Exercise E

Part A

Building sentences by using connectives. Below are 10 pairs of sentences. Begin the second sentence in each pair with the **connective** in parentheses. Use capital letters and commas. Write both sentences on the line. The first one has been done for you.

Common Connectives

as a result	in addition	nevertheless
consequently	moreover	

1. Pa was afraid that Grandma's house would fall down. He asked her to live with us. (consequently)

   Pa was afraid that Grandma's house would fall down. Consequently, he asked her to live with us.

2. Grandma's roof was ready to cave in. She wouldn't let anyone fix it. (nevertheless)

   _____

   _____

   _____

   _____

3. Grandma didn't want to leave the house because she was born and married there. Her seven children were born in the house. (in addition)

   _____

   _____

   _____

   _____

4. Pa took Grandma back to the old house. She was there during the terrible storm. (as a result)

_____

_____

_____

_____

5. The apple tree was very beautiful. It produced fruit that the family sold. (moreover)

_____

_____

_____

_____

6. The tree was very valuable to Pa. He refused to cut it down. (consequently)

_____

_____

_____

_____

7. The windstorm hit the apple tree. The tree was torn out of the ground. (as a result)

_____

_____

_____

_____

8. Shan and Mary didn't want to leave Grandma alone in the house. They went outside when she told them to leave. (nevertheless)

_____

_____

_____

_____

9. Grandma didn't feel comfortable living with us. She was homesick. (in addition)

_____

_____

_____

_____

10. Mom and Pa realized that the storm was dangerous. They got lanterns and hurried to the old house. (consequently)

_____

_____

_____

_____

Part B

Below is the **topic sentence** of a paragraph. Complete the paragraph.
Begin at least one sentence with a connective.

Grandma became very unhappy when she left her
house.

_____

_____

_____

_____

_____

_____

_____

_____

_____

_____

_____

_____

_____

_____

_____

Exercise F

Vocabulary review. Write a complete sentence for each word or group of words.

1. collapse _____

_____

2. income _____

_____

3. decaying _____

_____

4. crippled _____

_____

5. mournful _____

_____

6. surrounded _____

_____

7. clogged _____

_____

8. peril _____

_____

9. trimmed _____

_____

10. all at once _____

_____

SHARING WITH OTHERS

This section provides you with opportunities to share your thoughts and ideas with others, while you practice and improve your reading, writing, speaking, and listening skills.

Part A

Discuss the following questions. Share your answers with your partner or with the group.

1. At the end of the story, Grandma refused to move out of her house. Do you think she was right to stay, even though it was dangerous to do that? Explain.

2. Do you think Mom and Pa should have made Grandma move out of her house? Why?

3. Why did Pa decide to take Grandma back to her house?

4. Shan said that Grandma "had died where she wanted to die and maybe the way she had wanted to die." What did Shan mean? Do you agree? Explain why.

5. Were you surprised at what happened to Grandma? What clues in the story prepare the reader for the ending?

6. The word *sanctuary* means "a shelter, or a holy place." Why is the story called "The Sanctuary"? Think of another appropriate and interesting title.

7. Do you know someone who reminds you of Grandma? How is that person similar to Grandma? Discuss.

Part B

1. Suppose that you are Mom or Pa. On the lines below, carefully explain why Grandma should move out of her house. The purpose of your statement should be to convince.

_____

_____

_____

_____

_____

_____

_____

_____

2. Suppose that you are Grandma. On the lines below, carefully explain why you should remain in your house. Try to make your statement as convincing as possible.

_____

_____

_____

_____

_____

_____

_____

_____

_____

Part C
Poetry

LINEAGE

1. How many stanzas are there in the poem? How many lines are there in each stanza?

2. In "Lineage" the poet recalls, or remembers, her grandmothers. Which word does she most frequently use to describe her grandmothers?

3. The poet seems to be comparing herself to her grandmothers. What question does she ask at the end of the poem? How do you suppose the poet's life has been different from her grandmothers'?

THE COURAGE THAT MY MOTHER HAD

1. What do you think the poet admired most about her mother? What did the mother leave the poet? Did the poet value that? What would she have preferred?

2. Why do you think "The Sanctuary," "Lineage," and "The Courage That My Mother Had" were selected to appear together in a unit?

THE LADY OR THE TIGER?

based on a story by Frank Stockton

Before You Read

Connections

Read the title and study the picture on the left. Describe what you see.

- Who is the man standing with his arm raised? Notice his clothes and the chair behind him. What do these things tell you about him?
- Why is the young man in the center dressed the way he is?
- Who do you think the woman is? Where is the tiger?
- Do you like stories that take place in ancient times? Why or why not?

As you read, think about how the picture connects to the story.

Words to Learn

In this story, you will learn some new words. You will also learn an idiom. For example, *took his time* is an idiom that means "did not hurry."

THE LADY OR THE TIGER?

based on a story by Frank Stockton

It was a life-or-death decision.

Many years ago there lived a cruel and savage king. This king had a wild and violent imagination, and since he was king, he had the power to make his wishes come true.

The king loved to discuss things with himself. When he and himself agreed on something, the king commanded that it be done, and it was done at once because everyone in the kingdom was afraid of the king.

When things went smoothly, the king was pleasant and calm. But when a problem arose, his eyes gleamed and he rubbed his hands together with glee since there was nothing he loved more than correcting things that were wrong and destroying those who needed to be punished.

The king had heard about the public arena[1]—a place where men and wild animals could demonstrate their courage and strength by fighting each other. The idea appealed very much to this barbaric king. But he used it in a different way—to punish the guilty and reward the innocent.

Here is how it worked. When a man was accused of a serious crime, the king posted a notice. It said that on a certain day the man's fate would be decided in the king's arena. Everyone was invited to attend the trial.

The king's arena! Ah, how well it deserved that name! You see, the idea of an arena was not new, but the way it was used here was

1. *arena:* As used here, the word means "a large outdoor area where various events are held."

different, and came solely from the brain of the king. He thought of it because it delighted him and gave him pleasure.

On the day of the trial, a large crowd would gather in the king's arena. After everyone was seated, the king entered, followed by his court.[2] The king sat on his royal throne on one side of the arena. When the king gave a signal, a door would open and the accused man would step out into the arena. Opposite him, on the other side of the arena, were two doors, exactly alike and side by side.

The person on trial would walk to these doors and open one of them. He could open either door he pleased. No one spoke to him or offered any advice. The choice was his own.

Behind one of the doors was a hungry tiger, the fiercest and most cruel that could be found. If the man opened *that* door, the tiger immediately leaped out and tore the man to pieces. That was the punishment for his guilt! Then iron bells began to clang, cries of sorrow were heard, and the vast crowd, with heavy hearts, slowly made its way home. Everyone felt sad that the man had deserved to meet such a horrible fate.

But if the accused person opened the other door, a lady stepped out. She was as perfect a match for him as could be found in the land. The king nodded his head and singers and dancers came forward. Musicians played beautiful melodies on golden horns, and the two people were married at once. Then joyous bells rang out,

2. *court:* As used here, the word means "the people who serve, advise, and protect a king, queen, or other ruler."

the people shouted and cheered, and everyone threw flowers in the path of the innocent man as he led his bride to his home.

It didn't matter if the man already had a wife and family, or if he was in love with another lady. For as the king often said, "Nothing can interfere with my wonderful plan for punishing the guilty and rewarding the innocent."

The king was very proud of his way of administering justice. He thought it was perfectly fair. After all, the accused man could open either door he pleased. The choice was his. Of course, the man never knew whether he was going to be devoured or married, for sometimes the tiger came out of one door and sometimes out of the other. Still, the man's fate was in his own hands. And, in every case, justice was swift and final.

The plan was popular with the people too. They never knew what they were going to see. Would it be a bloody murder, or a joyful wedding? There was lots of suspense.

This savage king had a beautiful daughter. She was as wild and reckless as her father and, as you might expect, he loved her very much. As I have said, the princess was reckless. She was so reckless she fell in love with one of the king's servants. And though he was handsome and brave, he was, after all, only a servant. Still he loved her very dearly.

Their love affair went on happily for many months. And then one day the king happened to discover its existence.

The king did not hesitate or waver for a moment. The young man was immediately thrown into jail, and a date was set for his trial in the king's arena.

This was, of course, an especially important occasion. The king, and all of the people, were very interested in how the trial would turn out. Never before had such a case occurred. Never before had a slave dared to love the daughter of a king!

The king sent out men to find the fiercest tigers in the land. At the same time the kingdom was searched for a young lady suitable in beauty and rank, so that the young man could have a fitting wife in case fate did not throw him to the tiger.

Of course, everyone knew that the slave was guilty of the crime with which he had been charged. He had fallen in love with the princess. Both he and she admitted this fact! But the king would not think of allowing this to stand in the way of the trial. No, nothing could interfere with the workings of his arena. He simply enjoyed it too much. Besides, it didn't really matter how things worked out.

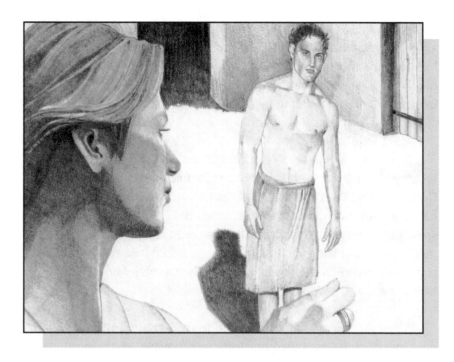

The young man would be murdered—or married—and in either case he'd be out of the way.

The great day finally arrived. People came from near and far, filling up every seat in the huge arena. Those who could not get in huddled together against the outside walls and waited for news.

The king entered and took his place on the royal throne. They were ready to begin. The king gave a signal. A door opened and the slave walked into the arena.

What a sight he was—tall, handsome, and proud! No wonder the princess loved him. What a terrible thing for him to be there!

The youth took his time as he walked across the arena. Then he turned and bowed to the king, for that was the custom. However, the young man was not thinking at all about the king. His eyes were staring at the princess, who sat next to her father.

From the moment the king had ordered her lover to appear in the arena, she had thought, day and night, of nothing else but this great event. The princess had more power and influence than any person who had ever been interested in a case. And so she did what no one else before her had ever done. She had learned the secret of the doors. She *knew* behind which door waited the tiger, and behind which door stood the lady. Gold and her power as princess had brought her the secret!

But she knew more than which door hid the lady. She also knew who the lady was! And she knew that the lady was one of the loveliest and most beautiful ladies in the king's court. She, alone, had been selected to be the wife of the youth, if he was found innocent of daring to fall in love with the princess.

Yes, the princess knew who she was.

And the princess hated her!

The princess had seen—or thought that she saw—the lady looking at her lover. And she thought he had even glanced back. Once, she had seen them talking together. It was only for a minute, it is true. But much can be said in a minute! Perhaps they were speaking about nothing at all. But how could the princess know that? The young lady was lovely—but she had dared to look at the princess's lover! So the princess hated the woman who silently waited behind the door.

When the young man turned and looked at the princess, his eyes met hers. He searched her face, which was paler than any in the ocean of faces around her. And then, as their eyes and souls met, he saw that she knew. She *knew*! She knew behind which door crouched the tiger, and behind which door stood the lady. She knew! He had expected her to know. He understood her, and he was certain that she would not rest until she had discovered the secret— the secret hidden to everyone else, even to the king.

The only way the youth could be sure of success was for the princess to discover the secret of the doors. And as he looked at her, he saw that she *had* discovered the secret, as he knew she would.

As he stared at her, his eyes burned with the question: *WHICH?* It was as plain to her as if he was shouting it to her from where he stood. There was not a second to lose. The question was asked in a flash. It must be answered in an instant!

The princess raised her hand and made a sudden, quick movement to the right. No one but her lover saw her. Every eye was staring on the man in the arena.

He turned and with a firm step walked quickly across the arena. Every heart stopped beating, every breath was held, every eye was on that man. Without the slightest hesitation, he went to the door on the right and pulled it open.

Now the point of the story is this: Did the tiger come out of that door, or did the lady?

The more we think about this question, the harder it is to answer. It means we must study the human heart—something that is very difficult to do.

Think about this. She was a wild and savage princess whose soul was burning with jealousy and hate. She had lost her lover. Should another woman have him?

How often, during the day and in her dreams, she had thought about the tiger leaping out with its cruel, sharp claws. Then she covered her face with her hands and was filled with horror.

But how much oftener she imagined him at the other door! She pictured his look of delight as he saw the lady. Her soul burned in agony as she saw him rush to the woman she hated. She could hear the glad shouts of the crowd and the bells ringing wildly. She imagined the priest marrying the couple right before her eyes, while she sat there helpless and in pain. Then she clenched her fists and tore her hair.

Would it not be better for him to die at once!

And yet—that awful tiger, those shrieks, that blood!

She had given her answer in an instant. But it had been made after many days and nights of anguished thought. She had known she would be asked. She had decided what she would answer. And without the slightest hesitation, she had moved her hand to the right.

Now the question I leave to you all is this: Which came out of the opened door—the lady or the tiger?

A traveler thinks about a difficult decision.

The Road Not Taken
by Robert Frost

Two roads diverged[1] in a yellow wood,
And sorry I could not travel both
And be one traveler, long I stood
And looked down one as far as I could
To where it bent in the undergrowth;   5

Then took the other, as just as fair,
And having perhaps the better claim,
Because it was grassy and wanted wear,
Though as for that the passing there
Had worn them really about the same,   10

And both that morning equally lay
In leaves no step had trodden[2] black.
Oh, I kept the first for another day!
Yet knowing how way leads on to way,
I doubted if I should ever come back.   15

I shall be telling this with a sigh
Somewhere ages and ages hence:
Two roads diverged in a wood, and I—
I took the one less traveled by,
And that has made all the difference.   20

1. *diverged:* went in different directions.
2. *trodden:* stepped on, trampled.

YOU CAN ANSWER THESE QUESTIONS

Put an *x* in the box next to the correct answer.

Reading Comprehension

1. Which sentence best describes the king?
   - ❑ **a.** He was kind and helpful.
   - ❑ **b.** He was cruel and wild.
   - ❑ **c.** He was loved by all.

2. The slave was thrown into jail because he
   - ❑ **a.** stole gold from the king.
   - ❑ **b.** fought the king's men.
   - ❑ **c.** fell in love with the princess.

3. Which statement is true?
   - ❑ **a.** The princess knew which door the lady was behind.
   - ❑ **b.** The princess liked the lady.
   - ❑ **c.** The princess had never seen the lady.

4. The princess moved her hand
   - ❑ **a.** to the left.
   - ❑ **b.** to the right.
   - ❑ **c.** at the young man.

5. The author asks the reader to decide whether
   - ❑ **a.** the young man deserved to die.
   - ❑ **b.** the lady or the tiger came out of the door.
   - ❑ **c.** the king's method of justice was fair.

Vocabulary

6. The king rubbed his hands together with glee. The word *glee* means
   - ❑ **a.** joy.
   - ❑ **b.** gloves.
   - ❑ **c.** soap.

7. Men could demonstrate their courage by fighting each other. The word *demonstrate* means
   - ❑ **a.** lose.
   - ❑ **b.** show.
   - ❑ **c.** run away from.

8. If he opened the wrong door, he was devoured by a tiger. The word *devoured* means
   - ❑ **a.** watched.
   - ❑ **b.** chased.
   - ❑ **c.** eaten.

9. The king let nothing interfere with his plan. The word *interfere* means
   - ❑ **a.** get in the way of.
   - ❑ **b.** talk about.
   - ❑ **c.** try to help.

Idioms

10. The youth took his time as he walked across the arena. The idiom *took his time* means
    - ❑ **a.** asked for more time.
    - ❑ **b.** ran very quickly.
    - ❑ **c.** did not hurry.

How many questions did you answer correctly? Circle your score. Then fill in your score on the Score Chart on page 184.

Number Correct	1	2	3	4	5	6	7	8	9	10
Score	10	20	30	40	50	60	70	80	90	100

Exercise A

Understanding the story. Answer each question with a complete sentence. You may look back at the story.

1. What happened when the king wanted something to be done?

   _____

   _____

2. What was behind one of the doors in the king's arena?

   _____

   _____

3. What was behind the other door?

   _____

   _____

4. Why was the king's arena so popular with the people?

   _____

   _____

5. With whom did the princess fall in love?

   _____

   _____

6. Describe the slave as he entered the arena.

   _____

   _____

7. Who was the lady behind the door?

   _____

   _____

8. How did the princess feel about the lady behind the door?

_____

_____

9. In which direction did the princess move her hand?

_____

_____

10. Which door did the young man open?

_____

_____

Exercise B

Adding vocabulary. On the left are 8 words from the story. Complete each sentence by adding the correct word.

throne

suspense

waver

custom

clang

administering

solely

existence

1. Since the people never knew what they were going

to see, there was lots of _____.

2. Iron bells began to _____

when the man was found guilty.

3. The idea of an arena was not new, but the

way it was used in the kingdom came

_____ from the king.

4. The king was very pleased with his method of

_____ justice.

5. The love affair went on for many months. Then the

king discovered its _____.

6. The king did not hesitate or

_____ for a moment.

7. The king entered the arena and sat on the

royal _____.

8. The young man turned and bowed to the king

because that was the _____.

Exercise C

Nouns with irregular plurals. Fill in each blank with the plural form of the noun in parentheses. These nouns have irregular plural forms. The first one has been done for you.

1. The king sent out _____*men*_____ to find the fiercest tigers in the land. (man)

2. The young lady was one of the most beautiful _____ in the king's court. (woman)

3. It didn't matter if the man already had a wife and

   _____. (child)

4. From near and far, husbands and _____ came to watch the trial. (wife)

5. The youth walked several _____, then bowed to the king. (foot)

6. The princess was so angry that she began to pull her hair and grind

   her _____. (tooth)

7. Years ago men fought wild animals in the arena. The men fought with

   their bare hands, without sticks or _____. (knife)

8. Outside the arena, _____ from the trees fell slowly to the ground. (leaf)

9. As the slave pulled open the door, the people in the arena were as

   quiet as _____. (mouse)

10. Nobody knows how many _____ were lost in the king's arena. (life)

Exercise D

Finding synonyms. Read each sentence. Then select the **synonym** (the word most similar in meaning) for the word in capital letters. Circle the letter of the correct answer. Each capitalized word appears in the story.

1. He was a cruel and savage king.

   SAVAGE   **a.** friendly   **b.** weak   **c.** fierce

2. When the king commanded that something be done, it was done at once.

   COMMANDED   **a.** hated   **b.** ordered   **c.** begged

3. The trials in the arena were very popular. Vast crowds came to watch.

   VAST   **a.** huge   **b.** small   **c.** strange

4. The princess was as reckless as her father.

   RECKLESS   **a.** good   **b.** wild   **c.** foolish

5. The princess had more influence than anyone in the kingdom except the king.

   INFLUENCE   **a.** power   **b.** friends   **c.** value

6. The princess thought that the lady noticed the slave and that he glanced back.

   GLANCED   **a.** called   **b.** looked   **c.** wondered

7. The people who could not get into the arena huddled together against the outside walls.

   HUDDLED   **a.** smiled   **b.** crowded   **c.** jumped

Exercise E

Part A

Building sentences. Combine two **simple sentences** into one **compound sentence** by using a comma and the coordinating conjunction (*but, and, or*) in parentheses. Write the compound sentence on the line.

1. He was a cruel king. He had the power to make his dreams come true. (and)

   _____

   _____

   _____

2. There was a lady behind one door. There was a hungry tiger behind the other. (but)

   _____

   _____

   _____

3. The man could open the door on the left. He could open the door on the right. (or)

   _____

   _____

   _____

4. The slave was thrown into jail. A date was set for his trial in the king's arena. (and)

   _____

   _____

   _____

5. Everyone in the arena was looking at the slave. He was looking at the princess. (but)

_____

_____

_____

6. Did the princess save the young man's life? Did she send him to his death? (or)

_____

_____

_____

Part B

Combine two **simple sentences** into one **complex sentence** by using the subordinating conjunction *(after, because, so that, until, when, why)* in parentheses. Decide whether the conjunction should be added before or after the first sentence. Add capital letters and commas, where needed. Write the complex sentence on the line.

7. A man was accused of a serious crime. His fate was decided in the king's arena. (when)

_____

_____

_____

8. The princess hated the lady. She saw her talking to the slave. (because)

_____

_____

_____

9. The king's method of justice was cruel. It was also popular. (while)

_____

_____

_____

10. The king learned about the slave. The slave was thrown into jail. (when)

_____

_____

_____

11. The princess did not rest. She found out which door hid the lady. (until)

_____

_____

_____

12. The princess had money and power. She was able to learn the secret of the doors. (so that)

_____

_____

_____

Exercise F

Vocabulary review. Write a complete sentence for each word or group of words.

1. interfere _____

   _____

2. devoured _____

   _____

3. clang _____

   _____

4. throne _____

   _____

5. suspense _____

   _____

6. custom _____

   _____

7. vast _____

   _____

8. huddled _____

   _____

9. existence _____

   _____

10. took his (or her) time _____

   _____

SHARING WITH OTHERS

This section provides you with opportunities to share your thoughts and ideas with others, while you practice and improve your reading, writing, speaking, and listening skills.

Part A

Discuss the following questions. Share your answers with your partner or with the group.

1. Why did the king think that his method of justice was perfectly fair? Do you agree with the king? Why?

2. Would such a method of justice be possible today? Explain.

3. Since he knew that the slave was guilty of the crime, why did the king insist that the trial go on? Give as many reasons as you can.

4. The author reveals that the princess "was as wild and reckless as her father." Why is it important for the reader to know this?

5. The princess hated the lady who was waiting behind the door. Suppose that the princess had liked the lady. Do you think that would have influenced the princess's decision? Why?

6. If you were the young man, which door would you have opened—the door on the left or the door on the right? Why?

7. Which came out of the opened door—the lady or the tiger? Refer to the story to support your answer.

8. Tell about a time you had to make a difficult decision.

Part B

1. On the lines below, describe the scene that occurred immediately
after the young man opened the door. Try to make your description
as *vivid* as possible.

_____

_____

_____

_____

_____

_____

_____

_____

_____

_____

_____

_____

_____

_____

_____

_____

_____

2. "The Lady or the Tiger?" is different from most stories because the reader, rather than the author, provides the ending. Did you like that unusual feature of the story? Did you find the story interesting? On the lines below, offer your opinion of "The Lady or the Tiger?" Begin with a topic sentence that tells whether or not you liked the story. Then give reasons to support your point of view.

_____

_____

_____

_____

_____

_____

_____

_____

_____

_____

_____

_____

_____

_____

_____

_____

Part C

Poetry

THE ROAD NOT TAKEN

1. How many stanzas are there in the poem? How many lines are there in each stanza? See if you can figure out the interesting rhyme scheme in this poem. (In each stanza, the first, third, and fourth lines rhyme with each other. The second and fifth lines also rhyme).

2. In "The Road Not Taken" a traveler thinks about a time when he had to choose between two roads. He makes the decision sound very important, yet he mentions that the roads were different in some ways and similar in other ways. Do you think the two roads are very different or quite similar? Support your opinion with quotations from the poem.

3. Read the poem again. Can it be that the poet is writing about more than just roads? Perhaps by taking a "less traveled road," he has decided to do something unusual or different. What do you think? What does the last line of the poem suggest?

4. In "The Road Not Taken" a traveler stands at a fork in a road and must make a decision. Why do you think this poem and "The Lady or the Tiger?" appear together in this unit?

THE SURVEYOR

by Alma Flor Ada

Before You Read

Connections

Study the picture on the left. Describe what you see.

- Who is the man in the chair?
- Who is hanging from the railroad tracks? How do you think he got into such a dangerous situation?
- What do you think the mood of the story is?
- What is the most exciting situation you have been in? Describe it.

As you read, think about how the picture connects to the story.

Words to Learn

In this story, you will learn some new words. You will also learn some idioms. For example, *to make fun of* is an idiom that means "to laugh at."

THE SURVEYOR

by Alma Flor Ada

The train was heading toward him, and there was no place to go.

My father, named Modesto after my grandfather, was a surveyor.[1] Some of the happiest times of my childhood were spent on horseback, on trips where he would allow me to accompany him as he plotted the boundaries of small farms in the Cuban countryside. Sometimes we slept out under the stars, stringing our hammocks between the trees, and drank fresh water from springs. We always stopped for a warm greeting at the simple huts of the neighboring peasants, and my eyes would drink in[2] the lush green forest crowned by the swaying leaves of the palm trees.

Since many surveying jobs called for dividing up land that a family had inherited from a deceased parent or relative, my father's greatest concern was that justice be achieved. It was not enough just to divide the land into equal portions. He also had to ensure that all parties would have access to roads, to water sources, to the most fertile soil. While I was able to join him in some trips, other survey-ing work involved large areas of land. On these jobs, my father was part of a team, and I would stay home, eagerly awaiting to hear the stories from his trip on his return.

Latin American families tend not to limit their family boundaries to those who are born or have married into it. Any good friend who spends time with the family and shares in its daily experiences is welcomed as a member. The following story from one of my father's

1. *surveyor:* a person who measures the size and shape of land.
2. *drink in:* an idiom that means "enjoy the sight of."

surveying trips is not about a member of my blood family, but instead concerns a member of our extended family.

Félix Caballero, a man my father always liked to recruit whenever he needed a team, was rather different from the other surveyors. He was somewhat older, unmarried, and he kept his thoughts to himself. He came to visit our house daily. Once there, he would sit silently in one of the living room's four rocking chairs, listening to the lively conversations all around him. An occasional nod or a single word were his only contributions to those conversations. My mother and her sisters sometimes made fun of him behind his back. Even though they never said so, I had the impression that they questioned why my father held him in such high regard.

Then one day my father shared this story.

"We had been working on foot in mountainous country for most of the day. Night was approaching. We still had a long way to go to return to where we had left the horses, so we decided to cut across to the other side of the mountain, and soon found ourselves facing a very deep, rocky valley. This gorge was connected on both sides by a railroad bridge, long and narrow, built for the sugarcane trains. There were no side rails or walkways, only a set of tracks resting on thick, heavy crossties[3] suspended high in the air.

"We were all upset about having to climb down the steep gorge

3. *crossties:* thick pieces of wood that support the rails of a railroad.

and up the other side, but the simpler solution, walking across the bridge, seemed too dangerous. What if a cane train should appear? There would be nowhere to go. So we all began the long descent . . . all except for Félix. He decided to risk walking across the railroad bridge. We all tried to stop him, but to no avail. Using an old method, he put one ear to the tracks to listen for vibrations. Since he heard none, he decided that no train was approaching. So he began to cross the long bridge, stepping from crosstie to crosstie between the rails, balancing his long red-and-white surveyor's poles on his shoulder.

"He was about halfway across the bridge when we heard the ominous sound of a steam engine. All eyes rose to Félix. Unquestionably he had heard it too, because he had stopped in the middle of the bridge and was looking back.

"As the train drew closer, and thinking there was no other solution, we all shouted: 'Jump! Jump!', not even sure our voices would carry up to where he stood, so high above us. Félix did look down at the rocky riverbed, which, as it was the dry season, held little water. We tried to encourage him with gestures and more shouts, but he had stopped looking down. We could not imagine what he was doing next, bending down on the tracks, with the engine of the train already visible. And then, we understood. . . .

"Knowing that he could not manage to hold on to the thick wooden crossties, Félix laid his thin but very strong surveyor's poles across the ties, parallel to the rails. Then he let his body slip down between two of the ties, as he held on to the poles. And there he hung, below the bridge, hanging down over the gorge but safely out of the train's path.

"The cane train was, as they frequently are, a very long train. To us, it seemed interminable. . . . One of the younger men said he counted two hundred and twenty cars. With the approaching darkness, and the smoke and shadows of the train, it was often difficult to see our friend. We had heard no human sounds, no screams, but would we have heard anything at all, with the racket of the train crossing overhead?

"When the last car began to curve around the mountain, we could just make out Félix's lonely figure still hanging beneath the bridge. We all watched in relief and amazement as he pulled himself up and at last finished walking, slowly and calmly, along the tracks to the other side of the gorge."

After I heard that story, I saw Félix Caballero in a whole new light. He still remained as quiet as ever, prompting a smile from my mother and her sisters as he sat silently in his rocking chair. But in

my mind's eye, I saw him crossing that treacherous bridge, stopping to think calmly of what to do to save his life, emerging all covered with soot and smoke but triumphantly alive—a lonely man, hanging under a railroad bridge at dusk, suspended from his surveyor's poles over a rocky gorge.

If there was so much courage, such an ability to calmly confront danger in the quiet, aging man who sat rocking in our living room, what other wonders might lie hidden in every human soul?

Put an *x* in the box next to the correct answer.

Reading Comprehension

1. The author's father was a
- ❑ **a.** lawyer.
- ❑ **b.** teacher.
- ❑ **c.** surveyor.

2. Why did Félix decide to walk across the bridge?
- ❑ **a.** That was the fastest way to go.
- ❑ **b.** He was afraid to go through the valley.
- ❑ **c.** Everyone encouraged him to go that way.

3. Why didn't the others try to walk across the bridge?
- ❑ **a.** They thought the bridge might fall down.
- ❑ **b.** It was faster to go through the valley.
- ❑ **c.** It was very dangerous to go that way.

4. When the train appeared, everyone urged Félix to
- ❑ **a.** run as fast as he could.
- ❑ **b.** wave at the engineer.
- ❑ **c.** jump off the bridge.

5. Félix saved his life by
- ❑ **a.** jumping into the river.
- ❑ **b.** hanging from the bridge.
- ❑ **c.** shouting until the train stopped.

6. Which phrase best describes Félix Caballero?
- ❑ **a.** boastful but weak
- ❑ **b.** quiet and courageous
- ❑ **c.** young and frightened

Vocabulary

7. The leaves of the palm trees were swaying in the breeze. The word *swaying* means
- ❑ **a.** moving.
- ❑ **b.** freezing.
- ❑ **c.** enjoying.

8. Everyone except Félix began the descent into the valley. The word *descent* means
- ❑ **a.** going up.
- ❑ **b.** going down.
- ❑ **c.** going alone.

9. Félix was able to confront danger calmly. The word *confront* means
- ❑ **a.** run away from.
- ❑ **b.** wish for or want.
- ❑ **c.** challenge or face boldly.

Idioms

10. Since Félix seldom said a word, they sometimes made fun of him. The idiom *to make fun of* means
- ❑ **a.** to laugh at.
- ❑ **b.** to learn from.
- ❑ **c.** to like.

How many questions did you answer correctly? Circle your score. Then fill in your score on the Score Chart on page 184.

Number Correct	1	2	3	4	5	6	7	8	9	10
Score	10	20	30	40	50	60	70	80	90	100

EXERCISES TO HELP YOU

Exercise A

Understanding the story. Answer each question with a complete sentence. You may look back at the story.

1. Who wrote "The Surveyor"?

   _____

2. What did the author's father do for a living?

   _____

3. How was Félix Caballero different from the other surveyors?

   _____

   _____

4. Why didn't all the surveyors walk across the bridge?

   _____

5. What method did Félix use to listen for the train?

   _____

   _____

6. How far across the bridge was Félix when he heard the sound of the steam engine?

   _____

   _____

7. What did the surveyors do when they saw the train?

   _____

8. How did Félix Caballero get out of the train's path?

   _____

   _____

Exercise B

Adding vocabulary. On the left are 8 words from the story. Complete each sentence by adding the correct word.

hammock

fertile

inherited

nod

solution

vibrations

suspended

interminable

1. It was easy to grow crops because the land

   was _____.

2. He put one ear to the track to listen for

   _____.

3. They wondered how to cross the valley. One

   _____ was to walk across the bridge.

4. He slept on a _____, which was tied

   between two trees.

5. Sometimes, children _____ land from

   a parent who had died.

6. Félix usually sat silently, but occasionally he would

   say a word or _____ his head.

7. The train seemed to go on forever; it was

   _____.

8. Félix was hanging down from the bridge,

   _____ from his surveyor's poles.

Exercise C

Part A

Using prefixes. **Prefixes** are letters that are added to the beginning of a word to change the word's meaning. Here are a few common prefixes:

Prefix	Meaning
un-	not
re-	again
mis-	bad

Add a prefix (*un-, re-,* or *mis-*) to the word in parentheses. Write the new word in the blank. The first one has been done for you.

1. Until we heard the engine, we were _____*unaware*_____ that the train was coming. (aware)

2. We were frightened, but Félix seemed calm and _____.
   (afraid)

3. Everyone shouted to Félix, but he was _____ to hear us.
   (able)

4. We stared at the smoke and waited breathlessly for Félix to

   _____. (appear)

5. The train had passed over Félix, but he was _____.
   (harmed)

6. When we climbed down into the valley, one of the men had the

   _____ to fall and break his arm. (fortune)

7. It took several months for the injured man to _____
   the use of his arm. (gain)

8. I was wrong about Félix; I had _____ the man. (judged)

Part B

Using suffixes. **Suffixes** are letters that are added to the end of a word to change the word's meaning. Here are a few common suffixes:

Suffix	Meaning
-able	able to be
-less	without
-ful	full of

Add a suffix (-able, -less, or -ful) to the word in parentheses. Write the new word in the blank. The first one has been done for you.

1. When the train headed toward Félix, the situation seemed

   _____*hopeless*_____. (hope)

2. Since there was nothing we could do to assist Félix, we felt

   _____. (help)

3. Félix had the strength to hang from the bridge because he was very

   _____. (power)

4. When we saw that Félix was safe, we were very _____.
   (joy)

5. Father could rely on Félix Caballero because Félix was

   _____. (depend)

6. Since the work was sometimes dangerous, one had to be

   _____. (care)

7. Félix was not afraid of anything; he was _____. (fear)

8. We liked visiting our grandparents. The time we spent with them was

   _____. (enjoy)

Now try this. Add a **prefix** and a **suffix** to the word in parentheses.

9. What happened to Félix was hard to believe; it was

   _____. (believe)

Exercise D

Finding synonyms. Read each sentence. Then select the **synonym** (the word most similar in meaning) for the word or words in capital letters. Circle the letter of the correct answer. Each capitalized word appears in the story.

1. Modesto made sure that everyone received an equal portion.

   PORTION　　　**a.** land　　　**b.** food　　　**c.** part

2. The children inherited the land because both of their parents were deceased.

   DECEASED　　　**a.** living　　　**b.** dead　　　**c.** ill

3. The only access to the lake was a narrow dirt road.

   ACCESS　　　**a.** entrance　　　**b.** railroad　　　**c.** boat

4. They did not want to climb down the deep gorge to get to the other side.

   GORGE　　　**a.** stones　　　**b.** valley　　　**c.** river

5. They were filled with fear when they heard the ominous sound of the train.

   OMINOUS　　　**a.** friendly　　　**b.** threatening　　**c.** calm

6. It was getting late and darkness was approaching.

   APPROACHING　　　**a.** annoying　　　**b.** leaving　　　**c.** coming

7. Her father liked Félix and held him in high regard.

   HIGH REGARD　　　**a.** foolishness　　**b.** worry　　　**c.** respect

8. Although they tried to stop Félix, their words were to no avail.

   TO NO AVAIL　　　**a.** helpful　　　**b.** useless　　　**c.** pleasant

Exercise E

Building sentences. You can make your sentences more powerful by using well-chosen **adjectives** and **adverbs**. Add the words in parentheses to the sentence. Write the new sentence on the line. The first one has been done for you.

1. Félix Caballero was a man who visited us now and then. (quiet, modest)

   Félix Caballero was a quiet, modest man who visited us now and then.

2. He liked to sit in one of the four rocking chairs. (silently, heavy)

   _____

   _____

3. A railroad bridge stood before us. (long, narrow)

   _____

   _____

4. No one wanted to climb down into that valley. (steep, rocky)

   _____

   _____

5. The train was heading in Félix's direction. (deadly, swiftly)

   _____

   _____

6. We looked at Félix, who was deciding what to do. (nervously, coolly)

   _____

   _____

7. The engine pounded, and steam filled the air. (furiously, gradually)

_____

_____

8. In the light we were able to see his figure hanging down from the bridge. (dim, lonely)

_____

_____

_____

9. I remember how Félix crossed that bridge, and how he saved his life. (treacherous, calmly)

_____

_____

_____

10. Félix's adventure taught me a lesson. (remarkable, valuable)

_____

_____

_____

Exercise F

Vocabulary review. Write a complete sentence for each word or group of words.

1. descent _____

_____

2. confront _____

_____

3. inherited _____

_____

4. nod _____

_____

5. ominous _____

_____

6. vibrations _____

_____

7. interminable _____

_____

8. high regard _____

_____

9. to no avail _____

_____

10. made fun of _____

_____

SHARING WITH OTHERS

This section provides you with opportunities to share your thoughts and ideas with others, while you practice and improve your reading, writing, speaking, and listening skills.

Part A

Discuss the following questions. Share your answers with your partner or with the group.

1. As a surveyor, Modesto's greatest concern was that "justice be achieved." What does this mean, and why was it important?

2. The author states that in Latin American families "any good friend who spends time with the family and shares in its daily experiences is welcomed as a member of the family." Offer your opinion on this point of view.

3. "You can't judge a book by its cover." What is the meaning of this old saying? Have you ever found this to be true? Discuss the circumstances. Explain how the saying applies to Félix Caballero.

4. When he heard the steam engine, Félix looked down and saw a rocky riverbed that had very little water. If the riverbed had been filled with water, do you think Félix would have jumped off the bridge? Give reasons for your answer.

5. If the same situation were to occur again, do you think that Félix would walk across the bridge? Would the other surveyors? Give reasons for your answer.

6. Have you ever done something dangerous or courageous? If so, tell what happened.

7. Read the last sentence of the story again. What do you think the author is saying?

Part B

Write a **composition** on the lines below. Call it "Something Dangerous" or "Something Courageous." Write about a personal experience or about someone you know. If you prefer, make up an experience.

IRREGULAR VERBS

Verb	Past Tense	Past Participle
be (am/is/are)	was/were	been
become	became	become
begin	began	begun
bring	brought	brought
build	built	built
buy	bought	bought
catch	caught	caught
cut	cut	cut
come	came	come
die	died	died
do	did	done
drive	drove	driven
eat	ate	eaten
fall	fell	fallen
find	found	found
fly	flew	flown
get	got	gotten
give	gave	given
go	went	gone
grow	grew	grown
have	had	had
hear	heard	heard
hold	held	held

Verb	Past Tense	Past Participle
keep	kept	kept
know	knew	known
leave	left	left
lie	lay	lain
lose	lost	lost
make	made	made
put	put	put
ride	rode	ridden
run	ran	run
say	said	said
see	saw	seen
sell	sold	sold
send	sent	sent
set	set	set
shake	shook	shaken
sit	sat	sat
sleep	slept	slept
speak	spoke	spoken
spend	spent	spent
steal	stole	stolen
strike	struck	struck
take	took	taken
teach	taught	taught
tell	told	told
think	thought	thought
throw	threw	thrown

Score Chart

This is the Score Chart for You can answer these questions.
Shade in your score for each part of the story. For example, if your score
was 80 for **Talking in the New Land**, look at the bottom of the chart
for **Talking in the New Land**. Shade in the bar up to the 80 mark. By
looking at this chart, you can see how well you did on each story.

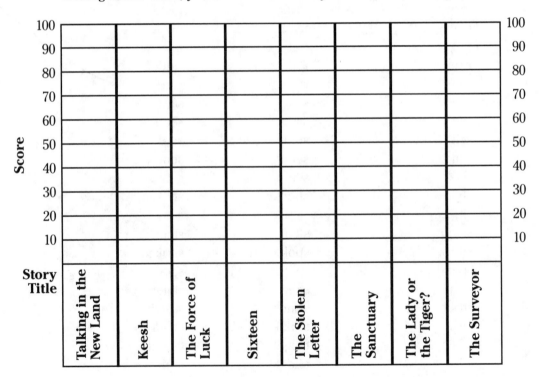